The Easiest Cookbook

Other books by Carol Guilford

THE NEW COOK'S COOKBOOK
THE DIET BOOK
CAROL GUILFORD'S MAIN COURSE COOKBOOK

The Easiest Cookbook

BY CAROL GUILFORD

J. B. LIPPINCOTT COMPANY
New York

Thanks to Hilda M. Rogers, who copy-edited the book with ultimate care and interest.

FIRST EDITION

Designed by Sally Baldwin and Ginger Legato

U.S. Library of Congress Cataloging in Publication Data

Guilford, Carol.
The easiest cookbook.
Includes index.
1. Cookery. I. Title.
TX715.G918 641.5 79-2587
ISBN-0-397-01366-3

---

79 80 81 82 83 10 9 8 7 6 5 4 3 2 1

To My Mother and Father

Contents

II. FISH AND SHELLFISH

III. CHICKEN AND OTHER POULTRY

V. PORK

VI. LAMB

VII. SIDE DISHES

VIII. DESSERTS

Introduction

One of the most complicated instructions in *The Easiest Cookbook* is to "slice an onion." For everyone who loves to cook well with a minimum of effort, this book is a collection of recipes requiring the simplest preparation.

I wrote *The Easiest Cookbook* while shuttling back and forth between home base, an apartment in New York City with a nice accumulation of kitchen equipment (my mother even sent a fish poacher one birthday), and the outfield, a transient apartment in Los Angeles, where my husband was working. In our L.A. kitchen, aside from a vibrant vista of the Hollywood Hills, the cupboard was bare. I had my travel can opener, a pocket pepper mill, and dozens of recipes to test.

I consulted *The New Cook's Cookbook,* curious to see how its author *(I)* expected *me* to set up a kitchen. Accepting some of my own advice, I invested in a large, heavy-bottomed skillet and a casserole roomy enough to double as soup kettle or spaghetti pot. A faithful friend gave me two sharply kept knives and a blender, its plastic container patched together with masking tape. I practically stole another friend's casserole—you know, the handy 1.893-liter size (2 quarts). My cousin dragged me to a discount barn to duplicate my Manhattan mixing and measuring essentials. I became the reluctant owner of twin tongs. Still, there was compensation in a pretty, practical, pottery baking dish.

Shopping and cooking on two coasts three thousand miles apart, I learned to appreciate the standard quality and availability of familiar products: a favorite brand of tuna packed in olive oil; smooth ice cream, churned without preservatives.

I recognized the easiest demand of creative cooking—taking advantage of fresh, local, regional produce. In New York, I am steps away from soft-shell crabs, in season whisked live from their Maryland bed, or sweet-meated pompano flown in from Florida. A subway ride to Greenwich Village means homemade Italian sausage, spiced like its Calabrian counterpart. In Los Angeles, I sauté native sand dabs and buy shiny-skinned summer squash in winter. What kind of chili powder to sample is a luxurious decision. And I smile a little because meat markets in L.A. sell "New York steak" and in New York they advertise "Western beef."

The world's exotic foods are everywhere. Exploring, I have seen Hungarian paprika in Boston, Japanese soy sauce in Dallas, Greek cheese in Richmond, and Rice Krispies in Guatemala City.

Food tastes best fresh, before it is condensed, dehydrated, frozen, chemicalized, or mixed with cream of mushroom soup.

The ingredients in this cookbook are as pure as possible. I have found no suitable substitutes for tart juice of lemon, the consistency of pressed olive oil, or the taste of real sweet butter.

The recipes and menus are designed for every day and party day, for the novice and the experienced cook, for all of us who consider our time and taste precious.

I. Appetizers

CREAM CHEESE AND SCALLION SPREAD
ELVIRA'S CROSTINI
AVOCADO CHUNKS • JOHN'S STUFFED
JALAPEÑO PEPPERS
GUACAMOLE • TORTILLA CHIPS
PÂTÉ WITH GHERKINS
GARLIC OLIVES • MARINATED MUSHROOMS
ROASTED PEPPERS AND ANCHOVIES
PEPPERONI AND PROVOLONE
MARINATED CHICK-PEAS • ARTICHOKE HEARTS
MORTADELLA AND GENOA SALAMI SESAME STICKS
EASIEST COOKBOOK GRAND ANTIPASTO
RED CAVIAR
RED CAVIAR DIP
AIOLI
CHEESE BOARD
"SUPERMARKET SPECIAL" CHEESE BOARD
FETA CHEESE • GREEK OLIVES • CHERRY TOMATOES
SMOKED SALMON
SMOKED WHITEFISH
HERRING
EASIEST COOKBOOK SMOKED FISH SUNDAY BRUNCH
FRIED MUSHROOMS
SOY-ROASTED CHICKEN LIVERS
QUICK BROILED SPARERIBS
CHINESE WRAPPED CHICKEN

An appetizer is a tempting tidbit eaten before the meal to whet the appetite—theoretically, anything from a peanut to fresh beluga caviar.

Appetizers are a daily affair for me, whether I'm home alone with a bowl of olives and the evening news or enjoying them my favorite way—for lunch, as Hors d'Oeuvres Variés, Antipastos, Tapas, First Course, or 熱 拼.

A memorable composition of appetizers was shared with friends after a languorous, sun-filled morning drive along the Côte d'Azur where France meets the Mediterranean Sea.

Three of us set out from Saint-Tropez, above us Nature's true blue sky, the one we knew lured the French Impressionist painters to come here and capture it on canvas.

History was beside us along the coast as we read each small signpost marking the World War II Allied invasion.

Winding our way up through the hills into Vence, we visited the Matisse chapel, pure white, plain, powerful, stirring.

Awaiting us at journey's end were the beautiful, bountiful serving boards and dishes of delicacies at the Colombe d'Or restaurant. Seated within view of a Calder mobile and next to a perfectly preserved thirteenth-century fireplace, we laughed, talked and ate, and ate.

Pâtés were brought to the table, one a coarse country style with big chunks of meat surrounded in gelée, another molded smooth and truffled.

The charcuterie, or sausage, followed, with smoked hams, garlic sausages, and a pot of mustard, one whiff of which was strong enough to revive a full faint.

There were marinated chick-peas, mushrooms, eggplant, artichoke hearts, and thumbnail-size Mediterranean mussels.

For dessert, the cheese board held Camembert and Roquefort.

To avoid gluttony, we divided an order of tiny spring strawberries and clinked brandy glasses, toasting our friendship with a promise to remember always our happy hours.

CREAM CHEESE AND SCALLION SPREAD

4 to 6 appetizer servings

The union of cheese and onion has been praised as far back as recorded history.

PREPARATION TIME: 15 minutes
COOKING TIME: None

2 8-ounce (227-g) packages cream cheese
½ cup milk
1 teaspoon Worcestershire sauce
6 to 8 scallions (green onions)

1. Soften the cheese at room temperature. Mash with a large fork, then whip in the milk and Worcestershire sauce. The mixture should be soft and spreadable. A food processor may be used.

2. Dewhisker and peel off the thin skin around the scallion bulb. Slice the scallions, including green tops, into ¼-inch (6 mm) pieces. Mix the scallions into the cheese. Chill until ½ hour before serving time.

Carol's notes: Serve on black bread or any thin, crisp cracker. Dip will keep in the refrigerator for several days.

ELVIRA'S CROSTINI

16 slices

Elvira Limentani, a woman of Rome and New York, taught me how to make this Italian cheese and anchovy toast.

PREPARATION TIME: 15 minutes
COOKING TIME: Under 5 minutes
BEST UTENSIL: Cookie sheet, or bottom of stove's broiling tray

1 *small loaf Italian bread*
¼ *pound (113 g) butter (1 stick), softened*
2 *teaspoons anchovy paste*
¼ *pound (113 g) mozzarella cheese, sliced thin*

1. Cut 16 ½-inch (1.3-cm) pieces from the loaf of bread. Mash together the butter and anchovy paste.

2. Arrange bread on a cookie sheet and broil in a preheated broiler 5 to 6 inches (13 to 15 cm) from the heat for 2 or 3 minutes or until the tops of bread are light brown.

3. Take out the tray with the bread slices. Turn. Liberally spread the anchovy butter on the unbrowned side of the bread, then cover each piece with slices of mozzarella cheese, cut to barely overlap the bread.

4. Return to the oven and broil 1 minute or until the cheese has melted.

Avocado Chunks *John's Stuffed Jalapeño Peppers*

AVOCADO CHUNKS

Allow 1 medium avocado for 2 or 3

PREPARATION TIME: 15 minutes
COOKING TIME: None

1 or 2 ripe avocados
(a ripe avocado yields to finger pressure)
Fresh lemon juice

1. Peel the avocado. The skin should slip off easily.
2. Cut avocado meat into mouth-sized chunks. Liberally squeeze on lemon juice. Serve on toothpicks.

Carol's note: Prepare as close to serving time as possible. Lemon juice will retard the avocado's darkening for at least an hour.

JOHN'S STUFFED JALAPEÑO PEPPERS

6 to 8 servings

Garbed in sombrero and multicolored serape, John Sous greets guests with peppers and tequila to celebrate the annual Mexican fiesta Cinco de Mayo (May 5).

PREPARATION TIME: 15 to 20 minutes
COOKING TIME: None

2 jars or cans Jalapeño peppers
(locate Jalapeños escabeche—pickled—where Mexican products are shelved)
½ pound (227 g) bleu cheese, softened
(soften at room temperature)
2 7-ounce (199-g) cans tuna, drained

1. Drain the peppers. Rinse quickly under cold running water. With a small, sharp knife, slit peppers down side without cutting completely through. Wash out seeds, then wash hands, as the seeds can burn the skin.

2. Stuff each pepper's pocket with hunks of the bleu cheese or the slightly mashed tuna. Arrange pinwheel fashion on a platter.

Carol's note: For a milder taste, use small, sweet "cherry" peppers.

Guacamole *Tortilla Chips*

GUACAMOLE

4 to 6 servings

Mexican avocado dip has come into its own. I haven't heard the question "What's that green stuff?" in a long time.

PREPARATION TIME: 15 to 20 minutes
COOKING TIME: None

2 *medium-sized ripe avocados*
(ripen avocados at room temperature; the perfect avocado is unstringy and slightly nut-flavored)
The following ingredients are adjustable to your own taste:
3 *or* 4 *tablespoons onion, finely chopped*
6 *drops Tabasco sauce*
2 *fresh lemons*
½ *teaspoon coarse salt*

1. As if cutting in half, slice the avocado lengthwise until seed is struck. Gently pull apart. Remove pit, then scoop avocado meat into a bowl.

2. Mash avocado by hand with a large fork, or very carefully in a food processor. The dip should not be too smooth. Tiny chunks of avocado should be visible.

3. Mix in the onion, Tabasco sauce, the juice of one lemon, and the salt.

4. Spoon into a serving bowl and squeeze juice from the second lemon on top to prevent darkening. Refrigerate until serving time.

Carol's note: Prepare Guacamole as close to serving time as possible.

TORTILLA CHIPS

Buy packaged tortilla chips or fry them up fresh.

PREPARATION TIME: 5 minutes
COOKING TIME: 1 minute per batch
BEST UTENSIL: 10-inch (25-cm) skillet

1 can tortillas
1 cup peanut oil

1. Cut the tortillas into quarters.

2. Heat the oil over medium-high heat until it sizzles. Carefully lay in 8 or 10 tortilla quarters. Fry for about 1 minute. The oil will stop sizzling when the chips are done. Remove chips from hot oil with tongs. Drain on paper towels.

3. Repeat the frying process until all tortillas are used.

Carol's note: Store in plastic bags.

PÂTÉ WITH GHERKINS

4 to 6 servings

A tin of pâté in the refrigerator is like a gold brick to set forth before unexpected visitors. An imported brand I see country-wide is "Alsace-Lorraine," made from pork liver and dotted with truffles.

Good gourmet food stores or departments sell pâté by the pound or by the kilogram.

PREPARATION TIME: 10 minutes
COOKING TIME: None

1 tin pâté
1 jar sweet gherkins

1. Chill the tin before serving. Rinse the tin with warm water before opening, then open both ends of the can. Gently push the molded pâté out onto a plate.

2. Accompany with a bowl of midget pickles and thinly sliced black bread or warm, crustless toast wedges.

Carol's note: For a light lunch, serve pâté on a pretty platter, surrounded with sliced tomatoes and cucumbers.

Garlic Olives *Marinated Mushrooms*
Roasted Peppers and Anchovies

GARLIC OLIVES

4 servings

An easy way to slip the skin from a garlic clove is to tap it lightly with a hammer. I demonstrated the method on a television show—or, tried to demonstrate it. I found myself standing between Steve Allen and Jerry Lewis, each equipped with his own hammer and garlic, which they tended to use for comedic rather than culinary purposes. I laughed a lot, but nothing got cooked.

PREPARATION TIME: 10 minutes
COOKING TIME: None

1 *pound (16 ounces, or 454 g) green olives, with pits*
4 *large garlic cloves, cut into quarters*
3 *lemon slices*
½ *cup olive oil*

1. Drain the olives from the jar or can. Rinse quickly under cold running water to remove brine. With a small, sharp knife, slit olives in three places. Slice down to pit to allow seasoning to seep in.

2. In a bowl, coat the olives with the garlic, lemon, and oil.

3. Marinate at room temperature at least 6 hours, then cover and chill. Drain ½ hour before serving. Save marinade for any uneaten olives.

MARINATED MUSHROOMS

4 servings

The good doctor for jarred or canned mushrooms.

PREPARATION TIME: 5 minutes
COOKING TIME: None

2 4-ounce (113-g) jars button mushrooms
2 tablespoons wine vinegar
2 tablespoons olive oil
A pinch (less than 1/8 teaspoon) of Coleman's dry mustard

1. Drain the mushrooms, then rinse them quickly under cold running water.

2. In a small bowl, mix the vinegar, oil, and mustard. A wire whisk is helpful to incorporate the mustard. Pour marinade over mushrooms. Coat well, then chill for several hours. To serve, pour off liquid and spear with toothpicks.

ROASTED PEPPERS AND ANCHOVIES

4 servings

PREPARATION TIME: 5 minutes
COOKING TIME: None

1 4-ounce (113-g) jar roasted peppers, drained (two good brands are Progresso and Mancini)
1 2-ounce (57-g) tin flat anchovies, drained
1 tablespoon red wine vinegar
1 tablespoon olive oil

1. Slice the peppers into wide strips or chunks. Arrange on a serving platter.

2. Lay the anchovy fillets on top of peppers. Drizzle the vinegar and oil over all.

Carol's note: Serve with thinly sliced Italian bread, or with cocktail forks and plates.

PEPPERONI AND PROVOLONE

6 servings

Pepperoni is long, thin, highly spiced Italian dry sausage. "Hot" pepperoni is flaked with red pepper.

The best provolone cheese is medium firm, has a pungent odor, and tastes a bit smoky.

PREPARATION TIME: Under 10 minutes
COOKING TIME: None

1 stick sweet pepperoni
1 stick hot pepperoni
½ pound provolone cheese

Arrange the cheese and sausage on a board or platter. Slice in advance or provide a sharp knife for diners to slice at their pleasure.

Marinated Chick-Peas *Artichoke Hearts*

MARINATED CHICK-PEAS

6 servings

Will answer to ceci beans or garbanzos.

PREPARATION TIME: 10 to 15 minutes
COOKING TIME: None

1 1-pound (454-g) can chick-peas
¼ cup red wine vinegar
¼ cup olive oil
½ teaspoon salt
1 teaspoon chopped sweet onion
⅛ teaspoon oregano
Freshly ground black pepper to taste

1. Drain the chick-peas well. While still in the can, refresh them by filling the can with cold water, then draining immediately.

2. In a medium-sized bowl, whisk together the vinegar, oil, salt, onion, oregano, and pepper. Pour over beans. Coat well. Marinate 2 hours, stirring occasionally, or overnight in the refrigerator.

Carol's note: Cocktail forks and plates are definitely needed.

ARTICHOKE HEARTS

3 to 4 servings

PREPARATION TIME: 10 minutes
COOKING TIME: 10 to 15 minutes
BEST UTENSIL: Small saucepot

1 9-ounce (255-g) package frozen artichoke hearts, partially defrosted
2 tablespoons water
1 clove garlic
1 thin slice lemon
¼ teaspoon salt

For the Marinade

¼ cup wine vinegar
¼ cup olive oil
½ teaspoon salt

1. Put the artichoke hearts into the pot with the water, garlic, lemon slice, and salt. Cover and steam for 10 minutes, or until they are just tender. Separate with a fork to speed cooking time. Drain well.

2. To make the marinade, whisk together the vinegar, oil, and salt. Pour over the warm artichoke hearts. Cool, then chill at least 2 hours. Drain and serve on toothpicks.

Carol's notes: Marinated artichoke hearts are available jarred.

As a hot side dish, cook and drain frozen artichokes, then season with butter, salt, and pepper.

MORTADELLA AND GENOA SALAMI SESAME STICKS

6 to 8 servings

Mortadella is a bologna-type sausage, sometimes studded with pistachio nuts.

Genoa salami is garlicky, slightly chewy, and dotted with cracked peppercorns. Best sliced fresh and thin.

PREPARATION TIME: 10 minutes
COOKING TIME: None

½ pound (227 g) Genoa salami
½ pound (227 g) Mortadella
Breadsticks
(with sesame seed, if possible)

Wrap each sausage slice around a sesame stick. Sausage will adhere. Arrange on a platter in pinwheel fashion.

Carol's note: Serve with a bowl of chilled black olives.

EASIEST COOKBOOK GRAND ANTIPASTO

The last seven recipes collectively transform themselves into an abundant first-course party buffet for eight.

MORTADELLA AND GENOA SALAMI SESAME STICKS
PEPPERONI AND PROVOLONE
ROASTED PEPPERS AND ANCHOVIES
MARINATED CHICK-PEAS MARINATED MUSHROOMS
GARLIC OLIVES
ARTICHOKE HEARTS

RED CAVIAR

Allow 1 or 2 ounces a serving

For the high price, settle for nothing but the highest quality.

Salmon roe should be plump and pink, neither artificially red-colored nor overly salty.

PREPARATION TIME: Under 10 minutes
COOKING TIME: None

2, 4, or 7 ounces red caviar
Lemon wedges
Chopped onions (optional)

1. Chill the caviar. Serve in its own jar, or use an attractive small bowl.

2. Serve with a plate of lemon wedges, a bowl of chopped sweet-tasting onions, and black bread.

Carol's note: Surround caviar with crisp sliced cucumber, or dot dollops in the center of cucumber slices (close to serving time).

RED CAVIAR DIP

4 servings

PREPARATION TIME: 15 minutes
COOKING TIME: None

4 ounces (113 g) red caviar
½ pint (227g) sour cream
4 tablespoons sweet onion, chopped

In a bowl, gently combine the caviar, sour cream, and onions. Mix gently to prevent the small eggs from breaking.

AIOLI

4 to 6 servings

Everyone in attendance must taste this Provençal garlic dip or back away from those who have.

PREPARATION TIME: 10 minutes
COOKING TIME: None
BEST UTENSIL: Blender

4 very large or 8 small-to-medium garlic cloves
3 egg yolks
¼ cup olive oil
1 tablespoon fresh lemon juice
½ teaspoon salt
½ cup olive oil

1. Put the garlic, egg yolks, ¼ cup oil, lemon juice, and salt into the blender container. Cover and whirl for a few seconds until mixture is smooth.

2. Remove the lid from the blender and add the ½ cup olive oil in a slow stream. When the mixture is the thickness of mayonnaise and the oil is incorporated, it is done.

3. Spoon into a serving bowl. Choose from, and surround with:

Green beans—fresh-cooked or canned (vertical pack)
Cauliflowerets—raw, or steamed or boiled for 10 minutes
Strips of carrots, celery, green pepper, and cucumber
Raw, cooked, or jarred mushrooms
Avocado chunks
Artichokes
Boiled new potatoes
Cooked shrimp

Carol's notes: For dinner, the sauce is good on any poached fish. Aioli will keep 2 or 3 days in the refrigerator, after which its garlic flavor deteriorates.

CHEESE BOARD

"Did you ever see orange milk?" retorted the counterman, when I asked if a hunk of cheddar I was considering was artificially colored.

All cheese starts with milk, and there are probably close to a thousand names for cheese but only twenty types, varying from creamy soft to crumbly to hard enough to grate.

A good store that cuts cheese from a wheel is an advantage, for sampling and for fully enjoying this desirable food.

CHEDDAR CHEESE

Try white Vermont cheddar or a sharp cheddar from New York State, natural cheddar from Wisconsin, or Tillamook, an Oregon special.

Carol's notes: Serve with thinly sliced onion, dark bread, and olives. For dessert, match with crisp, tart apples.

BRIE AND CAMEMBERT

Elegant soft cheeses, French in origin. When ripe and at full flavor, these cheeses have a runny center at room temperature.

Carol's notes: Serve with thin, crisp crackers. Doubles as dessert.

BLEU OR GORGONZOLA

Blue-veined cheeses. Very rich. "Baby" Gorgonzola is unveined, its flavor still subtle.

BEL PAESE

An Italian cheese. In Italian the name means "beautiful country." Semi-soft.

PORT SALUT

Strong-flavored semi-hard cheese first made by French monks.

KASSERI

Hard Greek cheese. Tastes a bit like good "eating" Parmesan.

"SUPERMARKET SPECIAL" CHEESE BOARD

In all major supermarket dairy refrigerators.

LIEDERKRANZ

An original American cheese. Creamy. Check date on box for ripeness. Borden does a nice job.

BONBEL

French. Semi-hard.

BRICK OR WEDGE OF NATURAL WHITE CHEDDAR

Good served with crackers, thinly sliced French or Italian bread, and a bowl of olives.

FETA CHEESE GREEK OLIVES CHERRY TOMATOES

4 servings

Good Greek feta cheese should not be too salty. A knowledgeable market refrigerates feta in its own brine and sells it by the chunk.

PREPARATION TIME: 5 minutes
COOKING TIME: None

½ *pound (227 g) Greek feta cheese*
½ *pound (227 g) black Greek olives*
1 *pint basket cherry tomatoes*
Coarse salt

1. Arrange the cheese on a board with the olives.
2. Wash the tomatoes, leaving stems on for easy pickup. Sprinkle with coarse salt. A little water left clinging to tomatoes allows the salt to stick.

Carol's note: Serve with pita or black bread.

SMOKED SALMON

4 or 5 servings

The American cocktail hour is, for me, a more festive time of day than the earlier English teatime, unless the hours collide.

The delicate gilt clock on the mantel chimed four. My hostess, ensconced in a graciously antiqued suite at a fashionable London hotel, ordered up "Tea for four," explaining, "The portions are so small, I order double everything."

It was a proper, quiet tea. We asked polite questions of each other as we nibbled at our carrot sticks and dainty cucumber sandwiches.

The gilt clock chimed five.

"Would you like a drink?"

"Yes. With ice! Can you order double ice here?"

"Uh-huh. They bring it in a silver cereal bowl. I'll get us something to eat, too."

The waiter twitched not a button on his stiff shirt as he removed the tea trays and returned, wheeling before him a room-service table that cradled a half-bottle of Beefeater's gin and four small plates of pale pink Scottish smoked salmon. There were four lemon wedges, four slices of thin, dark bread, and capers in a tiny pot.

Talk was fast, and laughter was loose.

Big Ben bonged six times as I stepped out into the London dusk, fortified by the customs of two countries.

PREPARATION TIME: Under 15 minutes
COOKING TIME: None

1 pound (454 g) Nova Scotia salmon, sliced thin (finest smoked salmon has a lean, velvety texture, is moist, unsalty, thinly sliced, and served cool, not cold)
Lemon wedges
Sweet onion, thinly sliced
1 tablespoon capers (optional)
Black bread

1. Carefully separate the salmon slices and arrange them on a large platter. Strew with well-drained capers. Decorate with lemon wedges.

2. Arrange the onion slices and black bread on a separate plate. Have a pepper mill handy.

Carol's note: "Lox" is heavily salted smoked salmon, traditionally eaten on a half bagel spread with cream cheese.

SMOKED WHITEFISH

6 to 8 servings

I serve it whole on a wooden board, decorated with lemon and parsley, to reveal it as a royal denizen of the lakes—and smokehouse.

PREPARATION TIME: 15 minutes
COOKING TIME: None

1 whole smoked whitefish, head and tail on
2 or 3 lemons, cut into wedges
Parsley or watercress, washed and dried
2 bunches scallions, dewhiskered and peeled
Coarse salt

1. With kitchen shears, carefully cut off the fish's entire top skin. (Later, during serving, when the top meat has been eaten down to the bone, turn the fish over and snip away the rest of the skin.)

2. Put on a board or a large platter. Garnish with the lemon and parsley or watercress. Serve the scallions on the side and coarse salt for the scallions.

Carol's notes: Guests help themselves and must be provided with plates and forks. Paper or plastic is advisable, as smoked whitefish is, to put it plainly, stinky.

Easiest to locate in a Jewish delicatessen. May be purchased in halves or slices. Chubs are smoked baby whitefish. Allow one per person for brunch.

HERRING

4 to 6 appetizer servings

Jarred herring fillets in wine sauce are more than passable. Serve solo on toothpicks, or fixed with fresh sour cream and onions.

PREPARATION TIME: 10 minutes
COOKING TIME: None

1 1-pound (454-g) jar herring fillets, packed in wine sauce
1 small sweet onion, thinly sliced
½ pint (227 g) sour cream

1. Drain the herring fillets.
2. Separate the onion into rings. Strew over herring fillets.
3. Spoon the sour cream over all. Mix gently.

Carol's note: For a simple supper, serve with hot boiled new potatoes.

EASIEST COOKBOOK SMOKED FISH SUNDAY BRUNCH

At high noon, await guests with Bloody Marys and Screwdrivers. Since smoked fishes are salty, pitchers of ice water will provide for the afterthirst. Beer is good too.

CREAM CHEESE AND SCALLION SPREAD

CHERRY PEPPERS, HOT AND SWEET

BLACK GREEK OLIVES

NOVA SCOTIA SALMON

Sliced onions, tomatoes

SMOKED WHITEFISH

Lemon wedges

HERRING

Black Bread Bagels

FRESH FRUIT

FRIED MUSHROOMS

4 servings

PREPARATION TIME: 15 minutes
COOKING TIME: Under 10 minutes
BEST UTENSIL: Large skillet

½ *pound (227 g) mushrooms*
3 *tablespoons sweet butter*
3 *tablespoons peanut oil*
2 *eggs*
Coarse salt to taste
Freshly ground black pepper to taste

1. Wash the mushrooms. Pat them dry, then cut off the tough stem bottoms. Cut mushrooms into thick slices. Beat the eggs and salt together in a bowl.

2. Heat the butter and oil in the skillet over medium-high heat. Dip mushroom slices into the beaten egg, then fry in the hot fat for 2 or 3 minutes on each side. Salt and pepper during the last minute of cooking.

3. Keep warm on a hot tray. Serve on toothpicks.

SOY-ROASTED CHICKEN LIVERS

4 appetizer servings;
2 main-course servings

PREPARATION TIME: 15 minutes
COOKING TIME: 15 to 20 minutes
BEST UTENSIL: Shallow baking dish

1 pound (454 g) fresh chicken livers
Japanese soy sauce

1. Rinse the livers under cold running water. Pat dry with paper towels. Cut each liver in half, slicing through the natural division.

2. Put the livers into a bowl and pour over them just enough soy sauce to bathe and coat.

3. Arrange liver in baking dish in one layer. Roast in a preheated 325° (163° C) oven, 15 minutes for a pink inside, 20 minutes for well done. Livers should be an attractive reddish-brown. Overcooking dries and toughens liver. Serve on toothpicks. Keep warm on a hot tray.

Carol's note: Convert into an Easiest Dinner with Easiest Rice, Bean-Sprout Salad, and fresh melon chunks.

QUICK BROILED SPARERIBS

4 to 6 appetizer servings

PREPARATION TIME: 15 minutes
COOKING TIME: 40 minutes

1 slab (3 to 4 pounds, or 1.4 to 2 kg) lean spareribs (have the butcher saw bones horizontally in two places to make 3 long strips, approximately the same size)

For the Marinade

½ *cup Japanese soy sauce*
Juice of 1 lemon
1 *teaspoon sugar*
2 *small garlic cloves, pressed*
2 *tablespoons Worcestershire sauce*

1. Slice the ribs in between each bone to make many small riblets.

2. Combine the soy sauce, lemon juice, sugar, garlic, and Worcestershire sauce in a large bowl. Add the ribs, coating well, and marinate anywhere from 1 hour to overnight in the refrigerator.

3. Drain off the marinade but save it for a basting sauce. Broil ribs skin side up 3 or 4 inches (8 to 10 cm) from heat, for 20 minutes. Baste once or twice. Turn ribs. Baste. Broil 20 more minutes, or until meat is sizzling. Baste once or twice. Ribs should be charred and crisp. Keep on a hot tray.

Carol's note: For an Easiest Dinner, bake potatoes along with the ribs and toss a salad.

CHINESE WRAPPED CHICKEN

4 to 6 servings

The summer stock theater's kitchen for cast and crew cooked inedibles. My friends and I, young and hungry actors, hiked to restaurant safety before, during, and after rehearsals. Invigorated by the brisk, almost autumn air, we ate up our salaries in a Chinese restaurant. Incongruously, eating with chopsticks and watching the New England yellow-red leaves fall in the surrounding wood, we called it "our out-of-the-way place in an out-of-the-way place."

Back in New York City, I re-created the recipe for Chinese Wrapped Chicken and served it all winter. Eaters unwrap foil packets to discover bite-sized, ginger-flavored breast of chicken.

PREPARATION TIME: Under 30 minutes
COOKING TIME: 30 minutes
BEST UTENSILS: Shallow oven-proof dish or cookie sheet; aluminum foil

2 *boned, skinned whole chicken breasts (4 pieces)*
½ *cup or more Japanese soy sauce*
2 *small cloves garlic, pressed*
Fresh gingerroot (about 1-inch [25 cm]-square piece)

1. Cut the chicken breasts into bite-sized pieces. Combine the soy sauce and garlic.

2. Dip chicken pieces in soy sauce, then place each piece on an ample square of foil. Top each piece with a sliver of ginger.

3. Wrap foil around chicken, package style. Twist ends to prevent leakage.

4. Arrange chicken packages in one layer on a sheet or shallow dish. Bake in a preheated 350° (177° C) oven for 30 minutes. Keep warm on a hot tray.

Carol's note: Quick dinner: Bake Easiest Rice along with the chicken.

II. Fish and Shellfish

RED SNAPPER ROASTED ON BAY LEAVES
EASIEST COOKBOOK CREOLE PARTY
LOUISIANA CRAB GUMBO
FOIL-ROASTED SMALL FISH
RAHN'S BAKED SOLE
GINGER STEAMED FISH
DEEP-FRIED FRESHWATER CATFISH
SWORDFISH MARINARA
TOMAS'S LEMON-CURRY FISH
SHRIMP WITH WINE AND CHEESE SAUCE
BAKED PEPPER AND GARLIC FISH STEAKS
JAMAICAN CODFISH
EASIEST COOKBOOK CHAMPAGNE LOBSTER DINNER PARTY
BROILED LOBSTER
BROILED TROUT WITH LIME BUTTER
SAND DABS AMANDINE
FIVE-MINUTE SCALLOPS
SHAD ROE WITH BACON
SOFT-SHELL CRABS WITH PIGNOLI
PICKLED SALMON
EASIEST COOKBOOK SHRIMP PEEL PARTY
UNCLE SAM'S SHRIMP PEEL

First, catch your fish store.

Passersby stop in front of the window of Citarella's fish market, sidestepping the fast flow of New York City's upper Broadway pedestrian traffic, to stare at a barrel of clear-eyed smelts, watch the lobsters lumber about the tank, or check the price of perch, printed in large letters on placards taped to the inside glass.

The day the octopus was perched on a bed of seaweed, each long tentacle stretched out, resting in a wooden crate of crabs, I elbowed my way through the outside crowd into the narrow, brightly lit store. A good fish store doesn't smell fishy, and I breathed in air redolent of the sea and the sawdust strewn around the wood-planked floor.

Along the length of the counter, mounds and mounds of shaved ice banked more varieties of fish than Baskin-Robbins has flavors.

Shrimp are sold in medium and large sizes, available raw in the shell, raw shelled, or cooked and shelled. Daily staples, for forty years now, have been fillets of sole or flounder, large whitefish and bass for baking, and plenty of panfish to fry, usually perch, porgy, and whiting. Fresh tuna, soft-shell crabs, shad with its roe, and button-size bay scallops appear seasonally.

There is a unique "takeout" clam service. One dozen littlenecks or cherrystones are opened to order, stacked in a red plaid cardboard box on layers of ice chips, then neatly wrapped and tied with string. The customer carefully carries the clams home, squirts them with lemon juice, seasons with a shot of hot sauce, and swallows.

The tempo at Citarella's is *presto.* To fill orders, boss Vinnie has the staff, white-aproned, stand ready with squares of wrapping paper to call out to the customers, "Next! Who's next?" During the after-work-hour rush, I've witnessed some impatient fish buyers clamoring for position.

I wait for my order near the cash register, the perfect lookout to observe the long wooden plank where the fish is scaled (with electric shears), cleaned, hosed down, boned, or filleted. If one wants a head or a tail left on a fish, best speak up, or *whack!* off it goes. From my vantage point, I can also see the big fish ready to be cut, brought in from the large refrigerators in the back.

Citarella's prompted me into trying many new fish recipes. Walking along on my way to daily neighborhood chores, I'd glance in the window and spot the flounders with the pretty yellow tails. That night I'd mix up 6 tablespoons of bread crumbs, 3 of olive oil, 1 of wine vinegar, spread the mixture on the white underside of two ½-pound flounders, then broil the fish for 10 minutes in a preheated broiler, 4 inches from the heat (no need to turn, serves 2, may be doubled), and serve.

The preceding meal can be prepared and cooked in 45 minutes, barely disturbing one's serenity.

If you discover a close-by source of regional and shipped-in fresh fish, you have found the main ingredient for fast, elegant, easiest menus.

RED SNAPPER ROASTED ON BAY LEAVES

2 to 4 servings

The bay perfumes the snapper and enhances the fish's delicate flavor.

PREPARATION TIME: Under 10 minutes
COOKING TIME: 20 minutes
BEST UTENSIL: Shallow oven-proof pan or dish

1 or 2 3-pound (1.4-kg) red snapper(s)
Bay leaves
Olive oil
Lemon wedges

1. Liberally line the pan with bay leaves.
2. Rub the fish's skin with olive oil, then arrange fish or fishes in one layer on the bed of bay leaves.
3. Roast, uncovered, in a preheated 425° (210° C) oven for 20 minutes. Serve surrounded with lemon.

Carol's note: Westerners can use Pacific red snapper fish fillets, cut thick. Allow ½ pound (227 g) per serving.

EASIEST COOKBOOK CREOLE PARTY

CHEESE BOARD

LOUISIANA CRAB GUMBO

Tabasco Sauce

RICE

DRY WHITE WINE

GREEN SALAD,
TOSSED WITH AVOCADO SLICES

PECAN CRACKER PIE

COFFEE, BRANDY, AND LIQUEURS

LOUISIANA CRAB GUMBO

6 servings

Creole gumbo is traditionally ladled into soup bowls. Hot rice is passed for diners to spoon in, along with Tabasco sauce for those who like it hot.

PREPARATION TIME: 15 to 20 minutes
COOKING TIME: About 45 minutes
BEST UTENSIL: Large top-of-stove casserole

- 1 *pound (454 g) fresh, frozen, or canned crab meat (pick out any cartilage)*
- ½ *pound (227 g) fresh okra, sliced into ½-inch (1.3-cm) pieces*
- 1 *medium onion (1 cup), chopped by hand or in a processor*
- 1 *1-pound (454-g) can whole tomatoes*
- 5 *cups (1.2 l) water*
- 1 *bay leaf*
- 3 *sprigs fresh parsley*
- 2 *teaspoons coarse salt*
- ½ *teaspoon dried thyme*
- ½ *teaspoon crushed cayenne pepper flakes*
- 1 *thin slice lemon*
- 2 *tablespoons butter*

1. Put the okra, onion, tomatoes, water, bay leaf, parsley, salt, thyme, cayenne, and lemon slice into casserole.

2. Bring liquid to a boil over medium heat, then reduce heat and simmer, uncovered, for 30 minutes, stirring occasionally. (The recipe may be made in advance to this point. Reheat liquid to boiling before adding crab.)

3. Add the crab to pot and simmer over low heat for 10 minutes. Add the butter. Cook 5 minutes more or until steaming hot. Stir frequently.

Carol's notes: For variation, 1 to 1½ pounds (454 to 681 g) shelled, deveined medium shrimp may be used. Recipe may be halved or doubled.

FOIL-ROASTED SMALL FISH

PREPARATION TIME: 15 minutes
COOKING TIME: 30 minutes
BEST UTENSILS: Shallow oven-proof dish; aluminum foil

1 1- to 1¼-pound (454- to 567-g) whole fish for each person: perch, porgy, whiting, etc.
Lemon juice
Coarse salt
Freshly ground black pepper
Thin lemon slices
Catsup
Butter

1. Freshen the fish by rinsing under cold running water. Pat dry. Squeeze the lemon juice over fish. Salt and pepper lightly.

2. Place each fish on an ample piece of aluminum foil. Stuff each fish's cavity with half a lemon slice. Lightly coat top of fish with catsup, about 1 tablespoon for each fish. Dot with butter, about ½ tablespoon per fish.

3. Fold foil around fish package style. Twist ends to prevent leakage. Arrange in one layer in the dish. Roast in a preheated 375° (190° C) oven for 30 minutes.

RAHN'S BAKED SOLE

2 to 4 servings

Single and sociable, Mr. White enjoys inviting friends to his favorite easiest company dinner.

PREPARATION TIME: 15 minutes
COOKING TIME: 20 minutes
BEST UTENSILS: Aluminum foil; shallow dish

2 to 4 medium-sized fillets of sole (1 to 2 pounds, or 454 to 908 g)
Coarse salt
Freshly ground black pepper
Garlic powder
Sweet basil (optional)
Butter
1 or 2 lemons, sliced
2 to 4 ounces (60 to 120 ml) dry white wine

1. Freshen the fish by rinsing quickly under cold running water. Pat dry. Lay each fillet on an individual, ample piece of aluminum foil.

2. Season fish with salt, pepper, garlic powder, and a few flakes of basil, if desired. Dot with butter (about ½ tablespoon per fish). Arrange the lemon slices on top. Pour in the wine, then fold foil securely around fish. Arrange foil packages in a shallow dish in one layer.

3. Bake in a preheated 375° (190° C) oven for 20 minutes. Rahn says, "Voilà!"

GINGER STEAMED FISH

2 to 4 servings

Chinese style. When the dish is done and the lid is lifted, breathe in and enjoy the aroma.

PREPARATION TIME: 15 minutes
COOKING TIME: Under 30 minutes
BEST UTENSIL: Large skillet with lid

- *1 or 2 2-pound (908-g) fishes, cleaned, with head and tail on (whiting, flounder, trout, bass, snapper, or an available favorite fish)*
- *Flour*
- *3 or 4 tablespoons soybean or peanut oil*
- *1 cup hot water*
- *¼ cup Japanese soy sauce*
- *¼ cup dry sherry*
- *½ teaspoon raw sugar*
- *2 tablespoons fresh gingerroot, peeled and cut into thin strips, or chopped*
- *2 to 4 scallions, including green part, sliced into 2-inch (5 cm) pieces*

1. Wash the fish under cold running water. Pat dry. Rub a little flour onto fish skin surfaces.

2. Heat the oil in skillet over medium-high heat. Add the fish or fishes and sauté for about 3 minutes on each side. Turn carefully with spatula and large spoon to avoid breaking skin.

3. Add the water, soy sauce, sherry, sugar, gingerroot, and scallions. Reduce heat, cover skillet, and simmer for 15 minutes.

DEEP-FRIED FRESHWATER CATFISH

4 servings

With its midnight-black color, frowning face, and curled whiskers, the catfish looks as fearsome as a showboat landlord foreclosing the mortgage. Yet the delicate taste and tender texture of the catfish is comparable to those of the graceful trout or the mighty silver-skinned salmon.

When I visit family in Missouri, where catfish is plentiful and respected, one night is always reserved "to go out and get Carol her catfish."

PREPARATION TIME: Under 15 minutes
COOKING TIME: About 10 minutes
BEST UTENSIL: Large skillet

4 *portion-sized whole catfish, heads off,*
or
4 *large or 8 small catfish fillets*
Milk, about 1 cup
Yellow cornmeal (start with 8 ounces, or 227 g)
Coarse salt
Freshly ground black pepper
2 *cups peanut oil*
Lemon wedges
Catsup, spiked with Worcestershire sauce and heated

1. Rinse the fish inside and out under cold running water. Soak fish in the milk for 15 to 30 minutes, turning every so often. Spread the cornmeal on a plate and season with salt and pepper.

2. Five minutes before cooking, drain milk from fish, then roll in cornmeal until evenly and heavily coated.

3. Heat the oil in the skillet over medium-high heat. When a small cube of bread browns in 45 seconds, the fat is ready, at 380° to 400° (193° to 204° C). Add the fish. Fry 4 or 5 minutes on each side until well browned. Turn carefully

with a spatula and a large spoon. If oil starts to smoke or pop, turn down heat. Serve garnished with lemon wedges and accompanied by catsup mix.

> **Carol's note:** This method of frying fish may be used with any small to medium panfish: whiting, flounder, porgy, butterfish, Virginia spot, or trout. Use white cornmeal for trout.

SWORDFISH MARINARA

4 servings

Marinara means "of the sea." This recipe is Spanish, recognizable by the use of sherry, Andalusia's pale amber gift to the world.

PREPARATION TIME: 10 minutes
COOKING TIME: About 30 minutes
BEST UTENSIL: 12-inch (30-cm) skillet with lid

- 2 *pounds (908 g) swordfish steaks, cut ½ to ¾ inch (1.3 to 1.9 cm) thick (any thick fish steak may be substituted)*
- 2 *tablespoons olive oil*
- *Coarse salt*
- *Freshly ground black pepper*
- 4 *8-ounce (227-g) cans tomato sauce*
- 1 *large (2 small) garlic cloves, pressed*
- 16 *small pitted green olives (optional; drain and rinse off brine)*
- 1 *cup dry sherry*

1. Rinse the fish quickly under cold running water. Pat dry. Rub surface of fish with the olive oil. Lightly salt and grind pepper over fish.

2. Put the tomato sauce, garlic, and olives into the skillet. Cook the sauce, uncovered over medium heat for 15 to 20 minutes. Sauce should barely bubble. Stir occasionally.

3. Stir in the sherry. Carefully lay in fish, spooning sauce over. Cover skillet and "poach-steam" over low heat for 10 minutes, or until fish is opaque. Taste to test for hotness throughout.

Carol's notes: The recipe may be halved. Good with Easiest Rice or boiled potatoes. Unusual, and very moist, served cold in summer.

TOMAS'S LEMON-CURRY FISH

2 to 4 servings

The Bluehaven Hotel was painted cotton-candy pink, bordered by turquoise sea and white sugar-spun sand, and set on a Caribbean island with zero restaurants. One ate at one's hotel, or didn't eat.

We listened to the hot rhythms of the steel band and stared at our plates of lukewarm slices of roast pork, the thin gravy slowly heading for the applesauce. The catering, we found out, was in tune with the tastes of the guests, most of whom were British.

Every now and then, during the next dreamlike days, shell searching along the shore or wandering back to our room at night, we caught a whiff of curry on the air—a mirage of scent, it seemed, since nothing resembling a spice had appeared on the hotel's dining table.

"The British *like* spices," I whined. "The British East India Company practically owned Bombay in the seventeenth century. Queen Victoria was crowned Empress of India in eighteen hundred seventy something. . . ."

On our last afternoon, as we waited for the sunset, the smell of curry was unmistakably wafted along with the sea breeze.

Determined to discover the source, we followed our noses toward a far side of the hotel, to a separate building hidden behind a green splash of thick foliage. It was the kitchen where food was prepared for the hotel's help.

An Alice in Wonderland door opened, and we saw Tomas, his tall, starched white chef's hat launched firmly on his black head.

"Have you got the curry?" I demanded, not meaning to sound frantic.

"Ah, we are cooking de big fish my brother William caught on his boat."

That evening, our last, while the hotel's other guests sipped consommé and cut into well-done roast lamb, a platter of Lemon-Curry Fish was set before us.

The room was suddenly scented with coriander and turmeric. Heads turned, noses lifted toward the pungent smell. The steel band played. We ate. For dessert, Tomas sent us brandied bananas. Later, when we thanked him, he said, "I should have liked to bring them to you on a flaming sword. We are proud of our native cooking."

The next year we read of strife on the island. The hotel was closed.

PREPARATION TIME: 15 minutes
COOKING TIME: 20 minutes
BEST UTENSIL: Shallow baking dish

2 to 4 small whole fish (heads off), approximately 1 to 1½ pounds (454 to 681 g) apiece: whiting, flounder, perch, or your favorite panfish
or
2 to 4 fish steaks, cut 1 inch (2.5 cm) thick
Olive oil
¼ cup fresh lemon juice
½ teaspoon imported Madras curry
2 small cloves garlic, pressed
1 cup hot water
1 large onion, peeled and cut into 8 pieces

1. Freshen the fish by rinsing quickly under cold running water. Pat dry. Lightly coat entire surface of fish with olive oil. Arrange fish in one layer in baking dish.

2. Wire-whisk together the lemon juice, curry, garlic, and hot water. Pour sauce over fish. Arrange the onions around and in between fish.

3. Bake, uncovered, in a preheated 350° (177° C) oven for 20 minutes. Eat hot or cold.

SHRIMP WITH WINE AND CHEESE SAUCE

4 servings

The wine is white; the cheese, Greek feta.

PREPARATION TIME: 30 minutes
COOKING TIME: About 30 minutes
BEST UTENSIL: Large skillet

1 to 1½ *pounds (454 to 681 g) raw, medium shrimp, peeled and deveined (allow 8 to 10 shrimp a person)*
1 *cup dry white wine (California Chablis is compatible)*
½ *pound (227 g) feta cheese (the less salty, the better: the best is preserved in brine and bought by the chunk; canned feta is refrigerator-stocked in some markets)*

1. Put the shrimp and wine into a bowl. Soak 5 to 10 minutes.

2. Crumble the feta cheese into skillet. Pour in white wine from shrimp.

3. Melt the cheese over very low heat. Stir frequently with a wooden spoon until cheese and wine are thick.

4. Add the shrimp, stir, and coat well. Sauce should barely bubble. Poach, uncovered, 15 to 20 minutes or until a

taste-tested shrimp is done. Stir occasionally during cooking time.

Carol's note: Serve with a lemon-oil dressed green salad, and sweet pastry for dessert. (Baklava, if available.)

BAKED PEPPER AND GARLIC FISH STEAKS

4 servings

PREPARATION TIME: Under 15 minutes
COOKING TIME: About 20 minutes
BEST UTENSIL: Shallow baking dish

4 fish steaks, about ½ pound (227 g) each (strong-tasting fish, such as carp or cod, respond well to this preparation)
4 large garlic cloves, chopped fine by hand or processor
1 teaspoon olive oil
Coarse salt
Freshly ground pepper
Lemon wedges

1. Rinse the fish steaks quickly under cold running water. Pat dry. Mix the chopped garlic with the olive oil, then spread garlic evenly over top surface (one side only) of fish. Lightly salt, then liberally grind on coarse black pepper.

2. Bake in a preheated 425° (218° C) oven for 20 minutes. If garlic has not browned, broil fish close to heat for 1 or 2 minutes. Decorate with lemon wedges before serving.

JAMAICAN CODFISH

4 to 6 servings

Two tablespoons of coconut oil is the unique secret to making this West Indian dish.

PREPARATION TIME: 15 minutes' soaking time
COOKING TIME: About 30 minutes
BEST UTENSIL: Medium-sized top-of-stove casserole

- 1 *pound (454 g) salted and dried codfish*
- 2 *tablespoons coconut oil (found where organic foods are sold, or in Spanish grocery stores)*
- ½ *cup sweet onion, thinly sliced*
- 1 *1-pound (454-g) can whole tomatoes*
- *Coarse salt*
- *Freshly ground black pepper*

1. Soak the dried cod in a bowl of cold water from 4 hours to overnight. Change water once or twice.
2. Pat the cod dry. Slice into 1-inch (2.5-cm) pieces.
3. Heat the coconut oil in casserole over medium heat. Add the onion and sauté, stirring frequently for about 5 minutes.
4. Add the tomatoes and cod pieces. Stir well. Reduce heat to low, and simmer, uncovered, for 20 to 25 minutes. Add salt and pepper to taste.

Carol's note: Traditionally served with rice or boiled potatoes and okra.

EASIEST COOKBOOK CHAMPAGNE LOBSTER DINNER PARTY

Your guests will know they're special.

PÂTÉ

Artichoke Hearts — Chilled black olives

BROILED LOBSTER

Butter Sauce

CORN-ON-THE-COB

Champagne

EASIEST COLESLAW

VANILLA ICE CREAM WITH GREEN CHARTREUSE

BROILED LOBSTER

2 to 4 servings

A cartoon comment on this American rarity pictured a large placard posted in a restaurant's window front advertising "All the lobster you can eat: $69.95."

PREPARATION TIME: Under 15 minutes
COOKING TIME: 15 to 20 minutes
BEST UTENSIL: Bottom of stove's broiler tray, lined with foil

2 to 4 1½-pound (681-g) lobsters, cleaned and split for broiling
(measure broiler to make sure it can handle 4)
½ to 1 pound (227 to 454 g) butter (2 to 4 sticks), melted
Fresh lemon juice
Lemon wedges

1. Arrange the lobsters meat side up in one layer in the broiler tray.

2. Brush lobster meat with a little of the melted butter, then squirt with lemon juice.

3. Broil in a preheated broiler 5 to 6 inches (13 to 15 cm) from the heat for 15 to 20 minutes. During last 1 or 2 minutes of cooking, lobsters may be raised closer to heat source. Wear cooking gloves or use pot holders.

Carol's note: Provide diners with individual small bowls of hot melted butter, and cocktail forks and nutcrackers, to deal with the claws.

BROILED TROUT WITH LIME BUTTER

4 servings

PREPARATION TIME: Under 15 minutes
COOKING TIME: About 10 minutes
BEST UTENSIL: Large, shallow baking dish or bottom of stove's broiler tray

4 *9-ounce (255-g) fresh trout, boned (head and tail on looks pretty)*
4 *ounces (113 g) butter (1 stick)*
Juice of 3 fresh limes (about ¼ cup)
½ *teaspoon salt*
1 *lime, quartered*

1. Rinse the trout quickly under cold running water. Pat dry. Arrange the fish in one layer. Dish or tray should be well greased with extra butter.

2. Melt the butter in a small saucepan. Stir in the lime juice and the salt.

3. With a basting brush, coat the inside and top skin surface of trout with the lime butter.

4. Broil 4 to 5 inches (10 to 13 cm) from the heat in a preheated broiler for 8 to 10 minutes. Baste after 4 minutes. Finished fish is opaque and falls into natural divisions when poked with a toothpick. (No turning is necessary.)

5. Pour over extra, reheated lime butter sauce. Garnish plates with the lime quarters.

Carol's note: Keep the meal easy with tiny boiled new potatoes and a lettuce, tomato, and cucumber salad.

SAND DABS AMANDINE

2 to 4 servings

Small, sweet sand dabs are native to California waters. Here's an Easiest butter-almond treatment for my Los Angeles friends.

PREPARATION TIME: 5 minutes
COOKING TIME: About 10 minutes
BEST UTENSIL: Large skillet

4 to 8 sand dabs, about 1 to 2 pounds (454 to 908 g) (fish is cooked with bone, which is easily removed by diner)
Coarse salt
2 to 4 ounces (57 to 113 g) butter (1 stick)
1 or 2 tablespoons peanut oil (oil delays butter from burning)
¼ to ½ cup almonds, slivered
Lemon wedges

1. Freshen the fish by rinsing quickly under cold running water.

2. Melt the butter and heat the oil over medium heat. When mixture is bubbly and sizzling (make sure it covers entire bottom of skillet), carefully lay in the fish.

3. Sauté 2 or 3 minutes on one side. Turn carefully with a spatula and a spoon. Add the almonds. Use the spoon to stir and coat them with butter. Sauté the fish 2 or 3 minutes more, or until the flesh falls into natural divisions when gently poked

with a toothpick or tines of a fork. Or taste. Serve as fast as possible, on hot plates decorated with the lemon wedges.

Carol's note: Serve with Shoepeg Corn Pudding and a platter of sliced tomato, cucumber, and avocado, drizzled with vinegar and olive oil and lightly salted.

Three Atlantic coast spring specialties, all top-of-the-stove quickies.

FIVE-MINUTE SCALLOPS

4 servings

PREPARATION TIME: 5 minutes
COOKING TIME: Under 5 minutes
BEST UTENSIL: Large skillet

2 pounds (908 g) bay scallops
4 ounces (113 g) butter (1 stick)
Coarse salt to taste
1 tablespoon fresh, chopped parsley (curly part only)
Lemon wedges
Pepper mill

1. Put the scallops into a strainer or colander and rinse quickly under cold running water. Pat dry with paper towels.

2. Slice the butter in 6 pieces, then melt in the skillet over medium heat. When the butter is bubbling hot, add the scallops. Cook and stir constantly for approximately 1 minute, depending on size of scallops. Taste for doneness. Stir in salt and the parsley. Spoon scallops and pan butter onto hot plates. Serve with lemon wedges. Allow diners to grind on their own fresh black pepper.

Carol's note: Recipe may be halved.

SHAD ROE WITH BACON

4 servings

PREPARATION TIME: 10 minutes
COOKING TIME: 10 minutes
BEST UTENSIL: Large skillet

12 slices bacon
2 medium-sized pair shad roe (4 pieces)
Coarse salt
6 tablespoons butter
Lemon wedges

1. Separate the bacon into slices. Arrange in a large shallow baking tray. One-half hour before serving dinner, bake in a 400° (205° C) oven for 20 minutes or until they are crisp. Drain on paper towels.

2. Carefully separate the pairs of roe by cutting membrane with kitchen scissors. Pat dry. Salt lightly.

3. Melt the butter in the skillet over low heat. (High heat will burst roe's membrane, spattering fish eggs all over the stove). Add the roe and sauté for 5 minutes on each side. Turn carefully with a spatula and a spoon. Arrange the roe on warm plates with lemon wedges and bacon slices.

SOFT-SHELL CRABS WITH PIGNOLI

2 to 4 servings

In spring, the crabs shed their hard shell.

PREPARATION TIME: 15 minutes
COOKING TIME: Under 10 minutes
BEST UTENSIL: Large skillet

3 to 5 *soft-shell crabs per person, depending on crab's size (average appetites can handle 4 or 5 tiny sweet crabs or 3 larger ones; be sure the fish market cleans them)*
Flour
2 to 4 *ounces (57 to 113 g) butter (½ to 1 stick)*
1 *tablespoon peanut oil*
Coarse salt
2 to 4 *small cloves garlic, chopped (optional)*
¼ to ½ *cup pignoli (pine nuts, available in small jars or loose in nut stores)*
Lemon wedges

1. Pat the crabs dry with paper towels. Flour both sides of crab just before cooking, as flour tends to sink into crab.

2. Heat the butter and oil in the skillet until hot and foamy. Use medium heat, as high heat will burst the crab.

3. Sauté shell side down first for 2 minutes. Shake skillet across burner if crabs stick. Salt lightly, then turn carefully with a spatula. Add the garlic and pignoli. Use a spoon to coat nuts and garlic with butter sauce. Cook crabs 2 minutes more, adjusting heat if necessary.

4. Spoon on sauce. Serve on hot plates with lemon wedges. The entire crab may be eaten.

PICKLED SALMON

4 to 6 servings

Tart-tasting, with a cool crunch of sweet onion. Serve on a summer's eve.

PREPARATION TIME: 15 minutes
COOKING TIME: Under 30 minutes
BEST UTENSIL: Large skillet with lid

4 to 6 fresh salmon steaks, cut ¾ to 1 inch (2 to 2.5 cm) thick
2 cups white vinegar
2 cups water
2 tablespoons pickling spices
2 tablespoons sugar
1 tablespoon salt
2 medium onions, thinly sliced

1. Freshen the salmon by rinsing quickly under cold running water. Pat dry. Arrange in one layer in a shallow dish.

2. Combine the vinegar, water, pickling spice, sugar, and salt. Pour over salmon. Marinate anywhere from 1 hour up to overnight in the refrigerator, turning fish once or twice.

3. Put the marinade and freshly sliced onions in the skillet. Bring liquid to a boil, then reduce heat to low. Lay in salmon. Cover skillet and poach 5 minutes. Turn salmon carefully, cover again, and poach 5 more minutes. (Liquid should barely bubble.) Uncover and cool salmon in marinade.

4. Chill. Serve each salmon steak with a portion of marinade and onions on top.

Carol's note: Pickled Salmon is also an excellent Easiest appetizer.

EASIEST COOKBOOK SHRIMP PEEL PARTY

GUACAMOLE
UNCLE SAM'S SHRIMP PEEL
HOT FRENCH BREAD
DRY WHITE WINE
HEAVENLY HASH CAKE
COFFEE

UNCLE SAM'S SHRIMP PEEL

6 servings

My uncle Sam's do-it-yourself evening. People peel their own shrimp, then dunk them, along with hot French bread, into a peppery, buttery sauce. My aunt mashes the Guacamole and delivers the dynamite Heavenly Hash Cake on page 194.

PREPARATION TIME: 15 minutes
COOKING TIME: 15 to 20 minutes
BEST UTENSIL: Large, shallow baking dish

Large or jumbo shrimp in the shell
(allow 6 to 10 shrimp per person, depending on size)
Freshly ground black pepper
¾ *pound (340 g) butter (3 sticks)*
About ½ teaspoon Japanese soy sauce
2 *small or 1 large loaf French bread*

1. Wash the shrimp well under cold running water. Pat dry with paper towels.

2. Arrange shrimp in one layer in pan. Liberally grind black pepper on top. Cut up the butter and distribute it evenly over shrimp. Sprinkle on the soy sauce.

3. Bake in a preheated 325° (163° C) oven 15 to 20 minutes, depending on size of shrimp. Peel and sample one to check.

4. Bake French bread alongside, sliced, but joined at bottom, then wrapped in aluminum foil.

Carol's note: For easiest serving, set shrimp on a serving table in a large bowl or a casserole. Spoon shrimp and butter sauce into individual soup bowls.

III. Chicken and Other Poultry

EASIEST ROAST CHICKEN
GILBERT'S CHICKEN IN THE POT
LEMON-GARLIC CHICKEN
OVEN-BARBECUED CHICKEN
OVEN-FRIED CHICKEN PARMESAN
JIM'S HONEY BAKED CHICKEN
CURRIED CHICKEN WINGS WITH YOGURT
JACK FU'S RED-ROASTED CHICKEN WINGS
CHICKEN KIEV
CRISPY DUCK
BROILED MUSTARD CHICKEN
FLORENCE SHUKAT'S CHICKEN AND MEATBALLS
EASIEST COOKBOOK CORNISH HEN PARTY
CORNISH HENS
POTTED TURKEY WINGS AND/OR LEGS
MR. LEE'S CHICKEN AND PEA PODS
CHICKEN FRICASSEE, PUERTO RICAN STYLE

The most magnificent market I never shopped in was empty, except for one preening rooster that was not for sale. The ruins of the Emperor Trajan's market in Rome, built at the beginning of the second century, are preserved well enough for the imagination to take hold.

The market was one of the splendors of the classical world, an ancient shopping mall, within it a forum, a temple, libraries, and the markets of 150 shops and stalls, some of them with bits of decoration still on the walls.

My friend Ann Marks and I were the only customers where once the noisy, hurrying, toga-garbed crowds stopped for flowers and perfume, took shoes to be repaired, or picked up a mixture at the druggist's.

We wandered through this bizarre bazaar, cycling up and down the spiral stairs, peeking into deep, narrow stalls, excitedly recognizing the wine and oil shops by the drain in the center of the floor. We walked the Via Biberatica (Street of Peppers), where that expensive spice was sold to the early Romans, who prized it. Inside the grand arcade, tiers of vacant shops no longer spilled with merchandise brought from the vast territory of the Roman Empire.

Across town, the Campo dei Fiori, an open-air street market, is alive with people, flowers, and food. One May morning, three days after a clumsy fall off a cobblestone curb in Naples caused me to sprain my ankle, I wrote in my travel journal:

> Warm enough for a cappuccino outdoors at a restaurant on the Piazza Navona. Limped around Rome. The trick is to step *on* the cobblestones, not slip in between them. Rehearsed and ready for the unabashed, curious Romans, explaining (cheerily) to all who asked about my foot and some who didn't, *"Sono caduta a Napoli."* ("I fell in Naples.")

At the Campo dei Fiori, I inspected every baby eggplant, cheese, and prosciutto in sight.

I bought some flowers, then stood on one leg and watched a woman transform artichokes into sculpture. Surrounded by her fresh farm vegetables, she held the artichoke high, turning it round and round with one hand while her other hand artfully circled the artichoke in the opposite direction with a paring knife, an action that removed the artichoke's thistly thorns from stem to tip. *Plop*—each artichoke dropped into a pan of water. (The vendors sell the ready-to-cook artichokes to restaurants.)

"Brava," I said, and explained in bad but getting-better Italian that I liked very much Italian *carciofi* because all was edible.

"Mi piace (I like) *carciofi alla Romana* (vinegar and oil) *e alla Giudea* (deep fried).

"Come ha fatto male il piede?" ("How did you hurt your foot?")

"Sono caduta a Napoli."

I was rewarded with an understanding nod.

At one o'clock the market disappeared, loaded up and driven away in pickup trucks.

I left, feeling the ghosts of the past creep back into the deserted piazza.

EASIEST ROAST CHICKEN

3 or 4 servings

"ERC" will slide right into your repertoire.

PREPARATION TIME: Under 15 minutes
COOKING TIME: Approximately 1½ hours
BEST UTENSIL: Small, deep roasting pan

1 3- to 4-pound (1.4- to 2-kg) roasting chicken
Rendered chicken fat (2 tablespoons) or olive oil or butter
Garlic powder
Coarse salt
Sweet Hungarian paprika

1. Rinse the chicken quickly, inside and out, under cold running water. Pat dry. If using chicken fat (recommended), pull out the yellow hunk of fat from chicken's lower cavity. Cut into small pieces, then melt over low heat in a small skillet.

2. Rub the chicken with the rendered chicken fat, olive oil, or butter, then freely sprinkle entire surface of chicken with garlic powder, salt, and paprika.

3. Roast the chicken, breast side up, in a preheated 350° (177° C) oven for 45 minutes. Breast skin will just begin to show signs of browning. Carefully turn chicken breast side down and roast 30 minutes.

4. Turn chicken breast side up once again. Increase oven heat to 400° (205° C) and roast 20 minutes more, or until chicken's skin is browned and crisp. Baste 2 or 3 times with the pan juices during the last 20 minutes.

Carol's note: The rendered chicken fat imparts a very special flavor to the chicken. Chicken fat may be bought separately and frozen.

GILBERT'S CHICKEN IN THE POT

3 or 4 servings

Gilbert Green and I have been collaborating cooks for many meals now (we met acting in the road company of the play *The Diary of Anne Frank*). We never cook without spirited disagreements, but one of our most peaceful, easiest efforts is this traditional way to stew a bird in its own juice.

PREPARATION TIME: 15 minutes
COOKING TIME: 2 hours
BEST UTENSIL: Large skillet or shallow top-of-stove casserole

1 3- to 4-pound (1.4- to 2-kg) chicken, quartered
Chicken fat
Coarse salt
Freshly ground black pepper to taste
Sweet Hungarian paprika
3 medium onions, thinly sliced

1. Rinse the chicken pieces quickly under cold running water. Pat dry. Cut off yellow fat globule from chicken's cavity, then slice into 4 or 5 small pieces. Season chicken with salt, pepper, and paprika.

2. Make a bed of the onions to cover bottom of cooker. Lay on the bits of chicken fat. Arrange the chicken in one layer, skin side up, on top of the onions.

3. Cover the pot and cook over very low heat for 2 hours. Check pot occasionally.

Carol's note: After 1 hour, if liquid is low, add ½ cup chicken broth.

LEMON-GARLIC CHICKEN

2 or 3 servings

Crisp and garlicky. Eat hot or cold. Doubled or tripled, the recipe for an Easiest company dinner.

PREPARATION TIME: 15 minutes
COOKING TIME: 1½ to 2 hours
BEST UTENSIL: Shallow nonstick pan, large enough to hold chicken in one layer

- 1 *3- to 4-pound (1.4- to 2-kg) chicken (have butcher remove backbone, then chop chicken into 16 to 18 pieces)*
- 5 *large garlic cloves, pressed*
- ½ *cup fresh lemon juice*
- 1 *tablespoon olive oil*
- 1 *tablespoon soy sauce*

1. Rinse the chicken quickly under cold running water. Pat dry. Arrange in one layer in pan.

2. Combine the garlic, lemon juice, olive oil, and soy sauce, then pour over chicken. (Chicken may marinate overnight.)

3. Bake the chicken, skin side down, for 1 hour in a preheated 400° (205°C) oven. Turn chicken with tongs. Bake chicken for 1 hour or until it is very brown and crisp.

Carol's note: To divide chicken into 16 pieces, remove backbone, then divide wings at natural joint (4 pieces), cut breasts in half (4 pieces), cut legs in half (4 pieces), and cut thigh portions in half (4 pieces).

OVEN-BARBECUED CHICKEN

4 or 5 servings

I grew up in Missouri, where the barbecue sauce is red, thick, and smoky.

PREPARATION TIME: 15 minutes
COOKING TIME: 1¼ hours
BEST UTENSIL: Shallow baking pan, large enough to hold chicken in one layer

- 2 *3- to 4-pound (1.4- to 2-kg) chickens, cut into 8 pieces*
- 1 *cup catsup*
- ¼ *cup Worcestershire sauce*
- 1 *tablespoon chili powder*
- 1 *tablespoon vinegar*
- ½ *teaspoon Wright's liquid smoke*
- ¾ *cup water*

1. Rinse the chicken quickly under cold running water. Pat dry.

2. Combine the catsup, Worcestershire sauce, chili powder, vinegar, liquid smoke, and water in a bowl. Use a basting brush to bathe chicken with a light layer of sauce.

3. Arrange the chicken, skin side up, in one layer in the dish. Bake in a preheated 350° (177° C) oven for 30 minutes, then turn chicken with tongs, baste well, and bake, skin side down, 15 minutes. Turn chicken skin side up once again and barbecue 30 more minutes, basting every 10 minutes.

OVEN-FRIED CHICKEN PARMESAN

2 or 3 servings

PREPARATION TIME: 20 minutes
COOKING TIME: 1 hour
BEST UTENSIL: Shallow baking pan

1 3- to 4-pound (1.4- to 2-kg) chicken, cut into 8 pieces
1 cup bread crumbs
½ cup Parmesan cheese, grated
(use processor, blender, or hand grater)
1 teaspoon salt
¼ teaspoon garlic powder
½ teaspoon paprika
4 ounces (113 g) butter (1 stick), melted
or
½ cup olive oil

1. Rinse the chicken quickly under cold running water. Pat dry.

2. Combine the bread crumbs, cheese, salt, garlic powder, and paprika.

3. Dip chicken into the melted butter or olive oil, then coat well with bread crumbs that have been spread on a plate.

4. Bake in a preheated 375° (190° C) oven for 1 hour. Chicken should be brown and crisp, with juices running clear when flesh is pierced with a fork's tines.

JIM'S HONEY BAKED CHICKEN

2 or 3 servings

Jim Field's fine fare.

PREPARATION TIME: 15 minutes
COOKING TIME: 1 hour, 15 minutes
BEST UTENSIL: Nonstick shallow roasting pan

1 3- to 4-pound (1.4- to 2-kg) chicken, cut into 8 pieces
or
Your favorite chicken parts
4 ounces (113 g) butter (1 stick)
½ cup honey
¼ cup prepared mustard
1 teaspoon salt
1 teaspoon curry powder

1. Rinse the chicken parts quickly under cold running water. Arrange in one layer in baking dish, skin side up.

2. Combine the butter, honey, mustard, salt, and curry powder. Mix well with a wire whisk. Pour over chicken and bake in a preheated 350° (177° C) oven for 1 hour and 15 minutes, or until chicken is tender and nicely browned. Baste every 15 minutes.

CURRIED CHICKEN WINGS WITH YOGURT

4 servings

Locate a fine, imported Madras curry powder.

PREPARATION TIME: 15 minutes
COOKING TIME: 1½ hours
BEST UTENSIL: Large casserole with lid

16 chicken wings
2 tablespoons curry powder
1 ½-pint (227-g) carton plain yogurt
½ cup water
1-inch (2.5-cm) piece gingerroot, slivered

1. Rinse the wings quickly under cold running water. Pat dry. Fold wing tips back.

2. Combine the curry powder, yogurt, water, and gingerroot.

3. Put chicken into the casserole. Pieces need not be arranged in one layer. Spoon over curry sauce, making sure all pieces are thoroughly coated. Cook, covered, in a preheated 325° (163° C) oven for 1½ hours.

Carol's note: Recipe may be doubled or tripled. Easiest Rice, steamed with white raisins and almonds, and a crisp cucumber salad are cooling consorts.

JACK FU'S RED-ROASTED CHICKEN WINGS

6 servings

PREPARATION TIME: About 30 minutes
COOKING TIME: 2 hours
BEST UTENSILS: Large skillet; large casserole

3 to 5 pounds (1.4 to 2.3 kg) chicken wings
Soybean or peanut oil
2 cups water
½ cup soy sauce
¼ cup dry sherry
¼ cup fresh gingerroot, slivered
2 large cloves garlic
4 scallions, cut into 1-inch (2.5-cm) pieces
2 tablespoons sugar

1. Separate each wing at the joint. (Try not to splinter the bone.) Rinse the wings quickly under cold running water. Pat dry.

2. Add just enough oil to the skillet to cover the bottom. Heat over high heat. When oil is hot, brown wings by stir-frying quickly for 4 to 5 minutes. Do this in batches of 20 pieces at a time to avoid crowding the pan. Add more oil if necessary.

3. Transfer all the chicken to the casserole. Add the water, soy sauce, sherry, gingerroot, garlic, and scallions. Stir

carefully. Bring liquid to a boil, then cover and simmer over low heat for 1 hour, stirring gently once or twice.

4. Add the sugar and cook 30 minutes more, or until wings are tender and meat is almost falling off the bone.

Carol's notes: Serve with rice and a Bean-Sprout Salad to complete the dinner.

For an appetizer, buy bean curd, souse it with soy sauce, then sprinkle over freshly chopped scallions.

CHICKEN KIEV

4 servings

Boned breast of chicken is rolled around a finger of butter, breaded, then fried fast and crisp.

PREPARATION TIME: Under 30 minutes
COOKING TIME: About 10 minutes
BEST UTENSIL: Large skillet

- 4 *small whole chicken breasts, skinned, boned, and halved (8 pieces)*
- 4 *ounces (113 g) butter (1 stick)*
  Coarse salt
- 1 *tablespoon snipped fresh chives, if available*
- 2 *large eggs, beaten with salt and pepper*
- 1 *cup bread crumbs, to start*
- 2 *cups peanut oil*

1. Flatten the chicken fillets with a wooden mallet or the bottom of a coffee mug. Put a butter finger, about ¾ inch wide and 2 inches long (2 by 5 cm), in the center of each piece. Sprinkle with coarse salt and the chives. Tuck in side flaps and roll, jelly-roll fashion.

2. Dip chicken rolls into the beaten egg, then into the bread crumbs, which have been spread on a plate. Repeat egg dipping and crumbing process. Let chicken set for at least 15 minutes. (This much may be done in advance.)

3. Heat the oil in the skillet until it is hot enough to brown a bread cube in less than 1 minute (or set electric skillet at prescribed temperature). Fry chicken for 4 to 5 minutes on each side, turning carefully with tongs. Drain on paper towels. If butter spurts when Kiev is cut, you've done it.

Carol's notes: The recipe may be halved. Serve with buttered noodles and hearts of artichoke salad.

CRISPY DUCK

4 servings

I have a few rare and interesting cookbooks. One, "A Treatise of all Sorts of Foods," was written by Louis Lémery, physician to King Louis XV of France.

The Lémery in my library is an English translation (from the French) published in London in 1745. More than two hundred years later, I found it in Paris at M. Edgar Soete's Librairie Salet, which specializes in rare cookbooks.

Here are Lémery's thoughts about duck:

> *Duck is nourishing enough and is a food that is solid and durable. Some authors think that the eating of it puts a good Colour into the Face, and makes the Voice pleasant and agreeable.*

PREPARATION TIME: Under 15 minutes
COOKING TIME: 8 hours
BEST UTENSIL: Large shallow roasting pan

2 5- to 6-pound (2.3- to 2.7-kg) ducks, halved (allow ½ duck per person)
Coarse salt
Freshly ground black pepper
Garlic powder
Sweet Hungarian paprika

1. Rinse the duck quickly, inside and out, under cold running water. Pat dry. Season liberally with salt, pepper, garlic powder, and paprika. Arrange in one layer in the pan, skin side up.

2. Roast duck in a 225° (107° C) oven for 8 hours. Pour off accumulated fat after 4 hours.

Carol's notes: The recipe may be halved.
Good with hot Chinese mustard, made by mixing dry mustard with water or beer.
Bake 6 to 8 raw eggs in their shell along with the duck. Eat as an appetizer, a snack, or breakfast.

BROILED MUSTARD CHICKEN

4 servings

A brown, juicy bird in Easiest style.

PREPARATION TIME: 15 minutes
COOKING TIME: About 45 minutes
BEST UTENSIL: Bottom of stove's broiler tray

2 2½-pound (1.1-kg) broiler chickens, split, backbone removed
4 ounces (113 g) butter (1 stick)
1 cup Dijon mustard
2 tablespoons Worcestershire sauce
2 tablespoons soy sauce
2 tablespoons catsup

1. Rinse the chicken quickly under cold running water. Pat dry.

2. Melt the butter in a small saucepan. Wire-whisk in the mustard, Worcestershire sauce, soy sauce, and catsup. Coat the chicken evenly with sauce. Marinate 1 hour, or overnight if possible.

3. Broil the chicken in its marinade in one layer as far from the heat as possible, about 7 to 8 inches (18 to 20 cm), in an electric stove.

4. Broil chicken skin side down for 20 minutes. Turn chicken carefully with tongs, then baste well with marinade–pan juices. Broil 20 to 25 minutes more, basting well every 6 or 7 minutes.

Carol's note: The recipe may be halved.

FLORENCE SHUKAT'S CHICKEN AND MEATBALLS

4 to 6 servings

PREPARATION TIME: 30 minutes
COOKING TIME: 2 hours
BEST UTENSIL: Large top-of-stove casserole

1 3- to 4-pound (1.4- to 2-kg) chicken, cut into 8 pieces
Coarse salt
Freshly ground black pepper
Sweet Hungarian paprika
½ cup water
1½ cups onion, chopped
1 tablespoon flour, mixed with ½ cup cold water

For the Meatballs

½ *pound (227 g) extra lean ground beef*
1 *large egg*
¼ *cup onion, grated*
(use processor, blender, or hand grater)
2 *garlic cloves, pressed, or ½ teaspoon garlic powder*
1½ *teaspoons salt*
⅛ *teaspoon freshly ground black pepper*
½ *cup plain bread crumbs*
½ *cup water*

1. Mix together the meatball ingredients in a large bowl. Roll and shape into golf-ball-sized meatballs (about 12). Cover until ready to use. May be made in advance.

2. Quickly rinse the chicken under cold running water. Pat dry. Season chicken pieces well with salt, pepper, and paprika. Put the ½ cup of water in the bottom of the casserole. Layer half the onions, half the chicken, then repeat layers, first onion, then chicken. Pour in flour-and-water mixture, then sprinkle with a bit of extra paprika. Bring liquid to a boil, then reduce heat, cover, and simmer over low heat 45 minutes.

3. After chicken has stewed 45 minutes, carefully arrange meatballs on top of chicken. Re-cover casserole and simmer slowly 1 hour and 15 minutes more.

Carol's note: The meatballs should "rest" about ½ hour before they go into the casserole with the chicken. Easiest to make them first.

EASIEST COOKBOOK CORNISH HEN PARTY

RED CAVIAR DIP

MARINATED MUSHROOMS

CORNISH HENS
on a bed of
SAUERKRAUT

ROSÉ WINE

CRANBERRY SAUCE

CAMEMBERT or
BRIE CHEESE
Crackers

CHOCOLATE-COVERED MINTS

CORNISH HENS

4 servings

PREPARATION TIME: 20 minutes
COOKING TIME: About 1 hour
BEST UTENSIL: Shallow roasting pan

4 *Cornish hens, about 1 pound (454 g) each (try to find them fresh, not frozen)*
4 *strips bacon, blanched (pork preferably, but beef bacon may be substituted)*

1. Rinse the hens inside and out. Pat dry. Salt lightly.

2. To blanch bacon, bring 2 cups of water to a boil in a small saucepan. Add bacon and simmer over low heat for 5 minutes. Drain bacon, then slice down center lengthwise, for 8 strips in all.

3. Arrange the hens in pan in one layer, breast side up. Crisscross each breast with 2 bacon strips. Roast in a preheated 350° (177° C) oven for 1 hour.

POTTED TURKEY WINGS AND/OR LEGS

4 servings

PREPARATION TIME: 20 minutes
COOKING TIME: About 3 hours
BEST UTENSIL: Large, deep roaster with lid

4 *large turkey wings, or legs, or any combination*
Rendered chicken fat or butter
Coarse salt
Garlic powder
Sweet Hungarian paprika
½ *cup red wine (any kind, dry or sweet)*
1 *medium onion, thinly sliced*
1 *rib celery*
1 *cup chicken broth*
4 *medium (portion-size) potatoes (optional)*
4 *carrots (optional)*

1. Rub the turkey parts with the melted chicken fat or softened butter. Season by sprinkling on salt, garlic powder, and a light coating of paprika.

2. Arrange the turkey in the roaster. Cook, uncovered, in a preheated 350° (177° C) oven for 45 minutes.

3. Pour on the wine. There should be an audible sizzle. Add the onion, celery, and chicken broth. Cover roaster. Reduce temperature to 300° (149° C) and cook for 2 hours and 15 minutes, or until turkey is very tender, almost falling from the bone. Add potatoes and carrots after 1 hour. When turkey is almost done (20 minutes before), pour off pan gravy and skim fat. Reheat. Serve in gravy boat.

MR. LEE'S CHICKEN AND PEA PODS

4 servings

Mr. Lee's restaurant, squeezed between the "Clothes Quarters" and McMary's Bar-B-Cue in a quiet suburb of St. Louis, practices the fine art of Cantonese cooking.

Mr. Lee explained this recipe to me at his restaurant over tea and fortune cookies.

PREPARATION TIME: Under 30 minutes
COOKING TIME: About 15 minutes
BEST UTENSIL: Large skillet

4 *whole boned, skinned chicken breasts (8 pieces)*
½ *pound (227 g) fresh pea pods (found in Oriental markets)*
½ *cup peanut or soybean oil*
½ *cup chicken broth*
⅛ *teaspoon cornstarch*

1. Rinse the breasts quickly under cold running water. Pat dry. Flatten breasts slightly with a mallet or a coffee mug's bottom. Cut the chicken into 1-inch (2.5-cm) cubes, slicing away any cartilage. Wash the pea pods, then pull off the thin string on each pod's underside.

2. Heat the oil over high heat. When a drop of water pops in the pan, add the cubed chicken and stir-fry (with a wooden spoon) constantly for one minute or until chicken becomes opaque. (Mr. Lee said, "When chicken changes color.")

3. Add the pea pods and stir-fry one minute. Add the chicken broth and sprinkle in the cornstarch. Stir well. Cover the skillet, reduce heat to medium low, and steam 4 or 5 minutes. Salt very lightly.

Carol's notes: Serve with soy sauce and hot Chinese mustard, a mixture of water or beer and dry mustard. Rice, tea, and chopsticks are appropriate.

To expand the dinner into a Far Eastern feast, add a second main course, Roast Pork Tenderloin with Bourbon and Soy.

CHICKEN FRICASSEE, PUERTO RICAN STYLE

3 or 4 servings

PREPARATION TIME: 15 to 20 minutes
COOKING TIME: 2 hours
BEST UTENSIL: Large top-of-stove casserole

3- to 4- pound (1.4- to 2-kg) chicken, cut into 8 pieces
2 tablespoons wine vinegar
¼ teaspoon garlic powder
½ teaspoon oregano
1 tablespoon coarse salt
¼ teaspoon freshly ground black pepper
1 small onion, thinly sliced
¼ cup olive oil
½ cup tomato sauce
1 tablespoon capers
12 small pimiento-stuffed olives

1. Quickly rinse the chicken under cold running water. Pat dry.

2. Combine the vinegar, garlic, oregano, salt, and pepper. Rub mixture into chicken. Marinate anywhere from 1 hour to overnight in the refrigerator.

3. Lay the onion in the bottom of the casserole. Pour over the olive oil and tomato sauce. Arrange chicken on top. Add the capers and olives. Cover and simmer over very low heat until chicken is tender (about 2 hours).

Carol's note: Good with boiled potatoes and a green salad.

IV. Beef

Being tired and hungry on a drizzling Friday evening in Paris without a dinner reservation is one of life's more pleasant problems. So it was bound to turn out well.

Chez Josephine, a restaurant I selected because of a favorable review in a back issue of *Gourmet* magazine, was booked solid.

We were almost out the door when the proprietor asked if we were English and how we had found his family-style small restaurant. Nodding his approval to our slow answers in halting, present-tense French, the owner remarked that the article in the American magazine had appeared some time ago. Would it be satisfactory, he continued, if a table for two was put up on the sidewalk in front of the open window outside the restaurant?

"Oui!" David and I said together.

Oui. Yes. *Oui.*

It was misting as the waiter held my chair and we took our places at a white-clothed table, one giant step from the side-street traffic of Paris.

We ordered *truffle en croute* ("fungus in crust" doesn't do it justice) and a bottle of house wine.

The ordering of the truffle (perhaps because of its high price) caused some commotion and chatter from two couples at the table next to us. By "the table next to us" I mean the table on the other side of the window, inside the restaurant.

It was raining lightly now. I buttoned my raincoat up around my chin.

The truffle arrived, looking beautiful and tasting superb, but it was enormous, orange-sized, very rich and filling. Our stomachs were not yet on schedule.

The waiters were very attentive, filling and refilling our wine goblets. One asked how we liked the truffle. The chefs wanted to know.

Our neighbors inside the window wanted to know if we were Canadian, what our professions were, and how we found this out-of-the-way neighborhood restaurant.

For an entree, we had ordered a Boeuf en Daube and a

cassoulet. Both dinners arrived in large earthenware casseroles. One main course would have fed the two of us.

The proprietor popped his head outside, felt the rain, and lowered a small awning over us.

We ate as much as we could. The beef in my pot looked dented, but David's dish was full of beans, nestling two long, fat, untouched sausages.

"I'm about to insult three waiters, two chefs, and a proprietor," he said.

"I'll put the sausages in my plastic rain hat."

With all the attention we were getting, it wasn't easy to sneak the sausages from the pot, wrap them in my rain hat, and secretly stuff them into my shoulder bag.

We had started to get silly but managed straight faces to refuse dessert, assure everyone dinner was *magnifique,* and promise that we would return.

The foursome in the window wanted the rest of our wine. I refused. I wasn't about to take the sausages and leave the wine.

A taxi ride later, we walked through the plush lobby of our hotel, I with two garlic sausages sticking out of the flap of my purse and David with a half-empty bottle of wine under his arm.

I put the sausage next to the spring flowers we had bought in the subway. I flushed them the next morning and threw the plastic rain hat (little beans clung to the accordion folds) into the wastebasket.

We spent all Saturday roaming and weaving through the thick crowds in Saint-Germain.

On our return to the hotel, we saw my plastic rain hat hanging on a towel hook in the bathroom.

Every day for a week I threw that rain hat into the wastebasket and each night found it retrieved, a reminder of our alfresco adventure at Chez Josephine.

BOEUF EN DAUBE

6 servings

An old French recipe for beef braised in wine, named for the three-legged vessel in which it was originally cooked. The calf's foot in the ingredients adds authenticity, flavor, and natural gelatin.

PREPARATION TIME: 20 minutes
COOKING TIME: 4 to 5 hours
BEST UTENSIL: Large top-of-stove casserole

- 5 *pounds (2.3 kg) lean beef chuck or rump, cut into 3-inch (8-cm pieces)*
- 1 *bottle dry red wine*
- 1 *medium yellow onion*
- 2 *large cloves garlic, chopped*
- 10 *peppercorns*
- 2 *slices bacon, blanched in boiling water for 5 minutes (see page 83 for bacon blanching instructions)*
- 1 *calf's foot, quartered*
- 1 *carrot*
- 1 *bay leaf*
- ¼ *teaspoon dried thyme*
- 2 *tablespoons salt*
- *Small piece lemon rind*
- 2 *tablespoons flour*

1. The beef may be marinated overnight in the wine, combined with the onion, garlic, and peppercorns.

2. Line the bottom of the casserole with the bacon. Arrange in the pot the calf's foot, beef, wine (reserve ½ cup), onion, garlic, peppercorns, carrot, bay leaf, thyme, salt, and lemon rind. Mix the flour with the reserved ½ cup wine and, when dissolved, add to the casserole.

3. Bring the liquid in the casserole to a boil on top of the stove, then bake covered for 4 to 5 hours or until the meat is fork tender. Skim fat from liquid. The gravy will not be thick.

Carol's notes: Serve with noodles and an Endive Salad.

The Boeuf may be made a day in advance. On the second day the flavor will be even richer. Warm the gravy first, then add the meat. Simmer over low heat until meat and gravy are hot.

The leftover beef may be jellied. Shred the beef and put it into a baking dish. Heat, then strain the gravy. Pour the gravy, laced with 2 tablespoons brandy, over the meat. Refrigerate overnight or until the liquid is jellied. Scrape off any fat, unmold, cut into squares, and serve.

BRAISED SHORT RIBS, BROWN GRAVY

4 servings

Rib bones give the gravy a deep, rich taste.

PREPARATION TIME: 15 minutes
COOKING TIME: 3 to 4 hours
BEST UTENSIL: Large, deep roaster with lid

4 to 5 pounds (2 to 2.3 kg) lean short ribs, or flanken (flanken is the German name for short ribs cut into narrow strips)
Salt
Freshly ground black pepper
Sweet Hungarian paprika
2 or 3 medium onions, thinly sliced
½ cup beef bouillon or dry red wine
Bay leaf
Garlic (optional)

1. Season the meat well by sprinkling on salt, pepper, and paprika.

2. Arrange a bed of onions on the bottom of the roaster. Lay the ribs on top of onions.

3. Add the bouillon or wine and the bay leaf. If you like, add 1 or 2 small cloves garlic.

4. Cover and roast in a 325° (163° C) preheated oven for 3 to 4 hours, or until meat is very tender. Turn after 1½ hours.

Carol's notes: If the gravy is too fat, pour off pan juices into a small pot ½ hour before roast is finished. Allow fat to rise to the top, then spoon off. Reheat the gravy before serving.

Nice with noodles and a romaine lettuce salad.

EASIEST MEAT LOAF

6 servings

A never-fail moist loaf for dinner, plus a built-in next-day sandwich on rye with hot mustard and pickles.

PREPARATION TIME: 20 minutes
COOKING TIME: About 1¼ hours
BEST UTENSIL: Shallow baking pan

- 2 *pounds (.9 kg) lean beef chuck, ground*
- 2 *eggs*
- 1 *6-ounce (170-g) can tomato paste*
- ¼ *cup chopped onions*
- ¼ *cup bread crumbs*
- 1 *teaspoon Worcestershire sauce*
- 1 *teaspoon soy sauce*
- 1 *teaspoon coarse salt*
- ¼ *teaspoon freshly ground black pepper*

1. Beat eggs with a fork in a large bowl. Mix in the tomato paste, onion, bread crumbs, Worcestershire sauce, soy sauce, salt, and pepper.

2. Add the ground beef. Mix well. For crusty, moist meat, shape into an oval loaf with wet hands. Bake in a preheated 325° (163° C) oven about 1¼ hours. Let rest 5 minutes, then slice.

EASIEST BEEF STEW

5 or 6 servings

The beef stews 5 hours while you do nothing, not even stir.

PREPARATION TIME: Under 30 minutes
COOKING TIME: 5 hours
BEST UTENSIL: Large deep casserole

- 2 *pounds (.9 kg) butcher's best chuck stew meat, cut into 2-inch (5-cm) cubes)*
- 1 *medium onion, coarsely chopped (1 cup)*
- 1 *cup fresh carrots, chunked*
- ¼ *cup green bell pepper, chopped*
- 3 *tablespoons tapioca*
- 1 *tablespoon sugar*
- 3 *tablespoons dry sherry*
- 1 *2-pound (908-g) can whole tomatoes*

1. Combine all ingredients in the casserole.

2. Cover and bake in a preheated 300° (149° C) oven for 5 hours. No stirring is necessary.

UNCLE DAVE'S PICKLED BEEF BRISKET

6 servings

Dr. Goldenhersh's aromatic way to mildly corn beef.

PREPARATION TIME: 15 minutes
COOKING TIME: 3 hours
BEST UTENSIL: Large soup kettle

1 5-pound (2.3-kg) brisket of beef
2 heaping tablespoons pickling spice
1 medium onion, quartered
1 or 2 cloves garlic
3 tablespoons coarse salt

1. Fill the kettle with enough water to cover the meat. Add the pickling spice, onion, garlic, and salt. Bring the water to a boil.

2. Carefully lay the brisket in the pot. Cover, reduce heat to very low, and simmer (the liquid should barely bubble) for 3 hours or until meat is tender when pierced with the tines of a fork. Cool beef in liquid. Slice thin to serve.

Carol's note: Serve hot or cold with boiled potatoes, horseradish, mustard, rye bread, pickles, and sliced tomatoes.

SKILLET STEAKS

2 to 4 servings

The easiest way to cook steak at home.

PREPARATION TIME: 5 minutes
COOKING TIME: Under 15 minutes
BEST UTENSIL: Large skillet

2 to 4 ¾-pound (340-g) steaks, cut 1-inch (2.5-cm) thick (shell [loin strip], tenderloin fillets, or rib steaks are choices)
Coarse salt
Garlic powder (optional)
Freshly ground black pepper (optional)
3 tablespoons olive oil

1. Lightly salt the steaks. Season both sides of meat with a sprinkling of garlic powder and/or freshly ground black pepper.

2. Heat the oil over high heat until a drop of water sizzles in the pan. Lay in the steaks and sear for 1 minute on each side or until meat is brown.

3. Lower heat to medium and cook steaks approximately 4 to 6 minutes for rare, 7 to 10 minutes for medium. Turn once or twice during cooking time.

Carol's note: As long as the steak fits in the pan, a large sirloin or porterhouse may be skillet-cooked.

EASIEST COOKBOOK ROAST TENDERLOIN OF BEEF DINNER PARTY

Entertain those who will appreciate your splurge.

SMOKED SALMON

ROAST TENDERLOIN OF BEEF

ANN'S POTATOES ANNA

DRY RED WINE

WATERCRESS AND SCALLION SALAD

CHOCOLATE MOUSSE

COFFEE BRANDY

ROAST TENDERLOIN OF BEEF

6 servings

A meat thermometer to check the internal temperature of the roast ensures perfection.

PREPARATION TIME: 5 minutes
COOKING TIME: 25 to 40 minutes
BEST UTENSIL: Shallow roasting pan with rack

6- to 8- pound (2.7- to 3.6-kg) beef tenderloin (trim top fat and reserve tail for another use)
2 or 3 tablespoons soy sauce
2 small garlic cloves, pressed (optional)

1. Bring the roast to room temperature.

2. Combine the soy sauce and garlic (if you wish) and spread over entire surface of meat.

3. Preheat oven to 425° (218° C). Insert meat thermometer into roast. Cook, uncovered, to 135° (57° C) for rare, 145° (63° C) for medium. Timing differs with each roast.

TAMALE BAKE

4 generous servings

PREPARATION TIME: 15 minutes
COOKING TIME: 1½ hours
BEST UTENSILS: Skillet; small casserole

1 pound (454 g) lean ground chuck
1 medium onion, chopped (1 cup)
2 tablespoons chili powder
1 1-pound (454-g) can whole tomatoes
½ cup yellow cornmeal
1 cup cold water
1 4-ounce (113-g) can chopped or sliced black olives
8 ounces (227 g) Monterey Jack or cheddar cheese, sliced thin (1 cup)

1. Put meat and onion in skillet (no fat is necessary). Cook over medium heat, browning meat until all red color is gone. Stir frequently.

2. Add the chili powder. Stir in. Then add the tomatoes, breaking them into small pieces with the edge of a large spoon. Cover the skillet and simmer 15 minutes.

3. Mix the cornmeal and water in a measuring cup or bowl. Add the cornmeal to the beef, which must be bubbling hot. Stir with a wooden spoon until mixture thickens (about 4 or 5 minutes). Mix in the olives.

4. Spoon into the casserole and bake, covered, in a preheated 350° (177° C) oven 55 minutes. Uncover and evenly spread the cheese over top. Bake, uncovered, 5 more minutes, or until cheese is melted.

HAMBURGERS

4 servings

An American treasure—grilled chopped-meat patties, fashioned after those at Melon's, a Manhattan West Side restaurant.

PREPARATION TIME: 5 minutes
COOKING TIME: Under 15 minutes
BEST UTENSIL: Skillet

1 pound (*454 g*) lean *ground chuck*
2 tablespoons cold water
1 tablespoon peanut oil
Coarse salt

1. Mix the ground meat with the water. Divide meat into 4 parts. Shape patties approximately 4 inches (10 cm) wide and ½ inch (1.3 cm) thick. Handle meat as little as possible. The water and light handling keep meat juicy.

2. Barely coat skillet bottom with the oil. Heat oil over medium heat. When a drop of water sizzles in the pan, add the burgers. Sear on each side for 2 minutes. Turn down heat and cook the burgers, about 5 to 6 minutes for rare and 8 to 10 minutes for medium. Turn with a spatula once or twice during cooking time. Sprinkle with salt to taste.

Carol's note: Serve on a plate or on hamburger buns. Have salt, pepper, sliced onion, relish, and catsup available.

CHEESEBURGERS

One minute before hamburgers are done, cover each with a slice of natural cheddar, Swiss, or mozzarella cheese. Cover skillet and cook until cheese is melted over top and side of burgers.

CHILI–CHEESEBURGERS

Heat a 16-ounce (454-g) can of your favorite chili (with or without beans). Spoon hot chili onto cheeseburgers.

BEEFBURGERS AU POIVRE

Crack whole peppercorns by whirling them in a blender until they are small flakes. Evenly coat surface of hamburger patties. Grill to desired doneness.

ON THE GRILL

Cook patties over a hot fire, close to the coals, for 5 minutes on each side for rare, about 7 minutes for medium, and 10 minutes for well done.

EASIEST COOKBOOK DO-NOTHING DELI PARTY

Allow ¼ pound (113 g) meat per person

Special only if the deli has correctly cured corned meats, tender, lean, and not too salty.

A delicatessen sure of itself will let you taste a sample sliver.

CORNED BEEF
PASTRAMI

RYE BREAD MUSTARD

RELISHES
POTATO SALAD
SAUERKRAUT
PICKLED PIMIENTOS

BEER

DILL AND SOUR PICKLES
COLESLAW
GREEN PICKLED TOMATOES
HOT CHERRY PEPPERS

CHEESECAKE
COFFEE

EASIEST BEEF STROGANOFF

4 servings

PREPARATION TIME: Under 30 minutes
COOKING TIME: 15 minutes
BEST UTENSILS: Medium-sized skillet; large skillet

2 *pounds (.9 kg) beef tenderloin*
2 *tablespoons sweet butter*
1 *small onion, finely chopped (½ cup)*
½ *pound (227 g) mushrooms*
1 *teaspoon dry mustard*
½ *cup beef broth*
⅛ *teaspoon Worcestershire sauce*
¾ *cup sour cream, at room temperature*
1 *teaspoon salt*
¼ *teaspoon freshly ground black pepper*

1. Make the sauce first. Melt the butter in the medium skillet over low heat. Sauté the onions and mushrooms for 5 minutes, stirring frequently. Stir in the mustard, beef broth, and Worcestershire sauce with a wire whisk. Simmer 3 minutes, stirring frequently.

2. Stir in the sour cream a little at a time. Add the salt and pepper. Heat must be low to prevent sour cream from boiling and curdling (separating). The sauce may be made in advance and reheated just before dinner.

3. Slice the beef tenderloin into 2- by 1-inch (5- by 2.5-cm) strips. Pat dry. Melt the butter in the large skillet over high heat. When fat is sizzling, sear the beef by stirring and turning to brown (about 2 or 3 minutes).

4. Add the meat to the sour cream sauce (which has been reheated to a slow bubble). Gently mix meat with sauce. Taste, and add more salt if needed. The dish is done when meat and sauce are piping hot.

Carol's note: Serve with noodles, and sliced beets marinated in oil and vinegar.

FILET MIGNON AU POIVRE (PEPPER STEAK)

2 to 4 servings

An elegant, Easiest, top-of-the-stove quickie.

PREPARATION TIME: 15 minutes
COOKING TIME: Under 15 minutes
BEST UTENSIL: Medium-sized skillet

2 to 4 filets mignons, cut 1 inch (2.5 cm) thick (filets mignons or tournedos are steaks cut from the small round end of the beef tenderloin)
1 to 2 tablespoons whole peppercorns
2 to 4 tablespoons brandy (cognac)
2 to 4 tablespoons Escoffier or A.1. Sauce
1 to 2 tablespoons butter
1 to 2 tablespoons olive oil

1. Pat the steaks dry. Trim all excess fat. Crack the peppercorns into small flakes by whirling them in the blender. Spread pepper flakes over both sides of steaks. Press pepper on with the palm of your hand.

2. Combine the brandy and steak sauce in a small bowl. Keep handy for later.

3. Heat the butter and oil over medium high heat. When a drop of water pops in the pan, add the steaks and sear for 1 minute on each side. Reduce heat to medium low and cook 6 to 7 minutes for rare and about 10 minutes for medium. Turn once or twice during cooking time.

4. Remove steaks from skillet to platter. Work quickly now. Add the brandy sauce mixture to skillet. Turn off heat. Vigorously stir together sauce and pan juices with a wire whisk. Pour over steak and serve.

EASIEST COOKBOOK CHILI PARTY

GUACAMOLE
or
AVOCADO CHUNKS

MONTEREY JACK
or
MILD CHEDDAR CHEESE

Tortilla Chips

CAL-TEX CHILI

CHILI BEANS

BLACK OLIVES

CHOPPED ONIONS

HOT PEPPERS

ICED CREAM

They know about chili in Los Angeles, and I have tried to sample the best of it, from Chasen's brothy meat and bean bisque (the chili's the best thing on or off the menu) to Barney's Beanery tomatoey stew.

At Barney's there are booths in between the pool tables and a choice of chili "straight" (without beans) or mixed with small red chili beans. Bowls of chopped onion and hot green chili peppers are free accompaniments. Grated cheese costs extra; no charge for stomach gas.

At Pink's Hot Dog Stand, the chili spread on the dog is spooned from a tall aluminum pot. Shredded and paste-thick, it appears to have slow-cooked on the back burner for a month. Happiness for me is this chili smothering a hot tamale.

The Magic Castle, a private club and refuge for magicians, makes a subtle-tasting, dark-colored broth with tender meat and beans. The price, as at Chasen's, is not subtle.

In the open-air cafeteria at Farmers Market, the fabulous complex of food stores and shops, I order the chili without beans at Stall No. 740, Bryan's Pit Barbecue. With my New York–trained eye sharp at spotting empty taxis and clean tables under umbrella canopies, I find a place in the sun to spoon up my spicy red ragout and watch the world go by.

CAL-TEX CHILI

6 to 8 servings

California chili with a touch of Texas, a composite from years of chili tasting. Make it the day before it is to be eaten.

PREPARATION TIME: Under 30 minutes
COOKING TIME: 4 hours
BEST UTENSIL: Large deep top-of-stove casserole

3 *pounds (1.4 kg) coarsely ground beef chuck (have the butcher grind the meat through the large-holed plate of the grinder, almost twice as large as for regular hamburger meat grind; find a meat market that understands)*
2 *medium onions, coarsely chopped*
2 *large garlic cloves, sliced*
6 *tablespoons chili powder (country-wide, the most available, reliable brand is Gebhardts)*
1 *teaspoon cumin seed*
1 *teaspoon oregano*
2 *teaspoons coarse salt*
2 *16-ounce (454-g) cans whole tomatoes*
2 *8-ounce (227-g) cans tomato sauce*
6 *drops Tabasco sauce*

1. Put the chili meat and onions in casserole (no fat is needed). Stir and cook over medium heat until all red is gone from meat. Add the garlic and chili powder. Stir well. Chili powder should coat meat.

2. Add the cumin seed and oregano, rubbing spices through your fingers as you add them. Add the salt, then stir.

3. Add the tomatoes (breaking them up with the edge of a large spoon), tomato sauce, and Tabasco. Stir. Bring the liquid to a boil, then reduce heat to low, cover the pot, and simmer 4 hours, or until meat is very tender.

Carol's notes: Cool, then refrigerate. To reheat, stir in ½ cup water, then warm, covered, over low heat. The recipe may be doubled.

QUICK CHILI

4 or 5 servings

Five stars.

PREPARATION TIME: 15 minutes
COOKING TIME: About 1 hour
BEST UTENSIL: Medium-sized top-of-stove casserole

1 pound (454 g) lean beef chuck, ground
2 tablespoons peanut or olive oil
1 medium onion, chopped (1 cup)
1 tablespoon chili powder
2 cloves garlic, chopped
1 teaspoon coarse salt
¼ teaspoon cumin seed
1-pound (454-g) can whole tomatoes, with juice
1 8-ounce (227-g) can tomato sauce
1 1-pound (454-g) can pinto or kidney beans, with juice

1. Heat the oil to sizzling over medium heat. Add the meat and onions. Cook, stirring frequently, until all red is out of meat. While meat is browning, break up into small pieces with a large spoon.

2. Add the chili powder, garlic, salt, and cumin seeds, which should be crushed between your fingers as you sprinkle them in. Stir well.

3. Add the tomatoes and tomato sauce. Stir, breaking up the whole tomatoes with edge of spoon.

4. Bring liquid to a boil. Add the beans, then turn down heat to low. Cover the pot and simmer chili for 45 minutes, stirring occasionally and checking to see that liquid is not bubbling too hard.

Carol's note: Recipe may be multiplied. Serve with grapefruit, onion, and avocado salad.

EASIEST COOKBOOK FONDUE BOURGUIGNONNE PARTY

GARLIC OLIVES MARINATED MUSHROOMS

ROASTED PEPPERS AND ANCHOVIES

FONDUE BOURGUIGNONNE

DRY RED WINE

ENDIVE SALAD

LEMON SOUFFLÉ

FONDUE BOURGUIGNONNE

A Swiss idea. Diners cook their own butter-soft cubes of beef tenderloin in a pot of sizzling oil, then dip the browned beef into a selection of sauces.

Proper equipment is necessary. A special fondue pot, equipped with a burner underneath, holds a can of Sterno. Electric fondue pots are available too. Fondue "plates" are divided into separate sections for meat and sauces. Forks for cooking the meat are long, slender, and two-tined.

PREPARATION TIME: About 30 minutes
COOKING TIME: Under 2 minutes
BEST UTENSILS: Fondue pot, plates, and forks

¾ *pound (340 g) beef tenderloin per person*
Sauces (choose two or more):
Barbecue sauce (see page 128)
Hot mustard sauce
(make sauce by mixing Coleman's dry English mustard with beer)
Soy sauce mixed with pressed garlic and ginger
Finely minced red onion
3 to 4 cups peanut oil
(fondue pot should be slightly more than half filled)

1. Trim all fat from the meat, then cut into neat ½- to 1-inch (1.3- to 2.5-cm) cubes.

2. Arrange the meat, sauces, and minced onion in separate sections on individual fondue plates. Meat must be at room temperature.

3. Just before serving, heat the oil in the fondue pot on the stove over medium heat. When oil is bubbling, carefully carry pot to the table to set on its stand over the heat source. (If oil cools during dinner, reheat on stove.)

4. Each person spears meat onto a fondue fork, then plunges it into the hot oil approximately 30 to 60 seconds for rare, 1 to 1½ minutes for medium, and 2 minutes for well done.

5. To eat, transfer meat to table fork, as fondue fork is tongue-burning hot, having been immersed in boiling oil. Dip cooked meat chunks into sauce or minced onion. Set coarse salt and a pepper mill on the table.

Carol's note: Fondue for two with candlelight and wine.

CORNED BEEF AND CABBAGE

6 servings

PREPARATION TIME: Under 30 minutes
COOKING TIME: About 4 hours
BEST UTENSIL: Large kettle with lid

4- to 5- pound (2- to 2.3-kg) corned beef brisket
1 medium onion, peeled and stuck with 4 cloves
1 large garlic clove
10 whole peppercorns
1 rib celery
1 bay leaf
6 medium-sized boiling potatoes, peeled
6 carrots, pared
1 medium-sized head cabbage, cored, washed, and cut into 6 wedges

1. Fill the kettle with enough water to cover the meat. Add the onion, garlic, peppercorns, celery, and bay leaf. Bring the liquid to a boil, then place the corned beef in the pot. Cover and simmer over low heat for 3 hours.

2. Add the potatoes and carrots. Cook, uncovered, for 45 minutes. Add the cabbage. Simmer 15 more minutes or until the cabbage is tender.

3. Turn off heat and allow beef to cool in liquid about 15 minutes. Slice beef lengthwise and arrange on a large platter surrounded by the vegetables.

Carol's note: Corned beef cured correctly is light in color (not dark red) and lightly salted. Provide horseradish, spicy mustard, and bread and butter. Beer is an appropriate beverage.

SALISBURY STEAK

4 servings

Below, a multiple-choice question:

Salisbury steak was named for *(a)* Salisbury, England; *(b)* J. H. Salisbury, a New York City socialite doctor specializing in obesity; *(c)* the Duke of Salisbury, who first served it at his table.

The correct answer is *b.* At the turn of this century Dr. J. H. Salisbury's Steak appeared on the ornate menu at Delmonico's Restaurant.

PREPARATION TIME: 10 minutes
COOKING TIME: 25 to 30 minutes
BEST UTENSIL: Shallow baking pan

2 pounds (.9 kg) lean ground sirloin or chuck, room temperature
1 egg
1 or 2 large garlic cloves, pressed
1 tablespoon coarse salt
⅓ cup water
Worcestershire sauce

1. Beat the egg with the garlic, salt, and water in a small bowl. Mix into the meat.

2. Shape the meat into an oval loaf. Lightly brush the top with Worcestershire sauce. (Meat must be at room temperature before cooking. Allow to stand unrefrigerated for 1 hour.)

3. Bake in a preheated 450° (232° C) oven for 20 to 30 minutes. When sliced, steak will be pink inside. For medium, bake no more than 5 to 10 minutes more.

Carol's note: Serve with Mushrooms in Soy.

OLD-FASHIONED POT ROAST

4 to 6 servings

With potatoes and carrots. Modernized with red wine.

PREPARATION TIME: Under 30 minutes
COOKING TIME: 3 to 4 hours
BEST UTENSIL: Large deep roaster with lid

3- to 5- pound (1.4- to 2.3-kg) pot roast (rolled and tied chuck roast or your pot roast preference)
Coarse salt
Freshly ground black pepper
Sweet Hungarian paprika
2 medium onions, thinly sliced
1 cup red wine
Bay leaf
4 to 6 carrots, pared
4 to 6 portion-sized (medium) potatoes

1. Season the roast all over with salt, pepper, and paprika.
2. Make a bed of onions in the bottom of the roaster. Pour on the wine, then add bay leaf. Place the meat on top.
3. Roast, covered, in a preheated 325° (163° C) oven for 3 to 4 hours or until meat is tender when pierced with fork tines.
4. Turn the roast after 1½ hours. Add the carrots and potatoes at the same time.
5. One-half hour before eating, turn roast again. Pour off gravy and skim surface fat. Reheat and pour into gravy boat to serve.

VEAL BREAST PAPRIKA

4 servings

If small, pink, lean veal ribs happen to run into you, take them home for dinner.

PREPARATION TIME: 15 minutes
COOKING TIME: 4 hours
BEST UTENSIL: Roaster with lid

2 3- to 4-pound (1.4 to 2-kg) breasts of veal
Coarse salt
Sweet Hungarian paprika
3 medium yellow onions, thinly sliced
½ cup catsup

1. Salt the veal, then sprinkle top surface with a heavy coating of paprika.

2. Make a bed of onions in the bottom of the roaster. Add the catsup. Arrange ribs on top.

3. Roast in a preheated 250° (121° C) oven for 4 hours or until meat is practically falling off the bone.

Carol's note: Serve with noodles and Cucumber Salad.

SMOKY CHUCK STEAK

4 servings

PREPARATION TIME: Under 15 minutes
COOKING TIME: 3 to 4 hours
BEST UTENSIL: Deep roaster and lid

- *3- to 4- pound (1.4- to 2-kg) lean chuck blade steak, cut 1 to 1½ inches (2.5 to 3.8 cm) thick (porous red bones and white, crumbly fat are signs of quality and freshness)*
- *½ cup water*
- *½ teaspoon Wright's liquid smoke*
- *1 teaspoon chili powder*
- *1 teaspoon garlic powder*
- *1 teaspoon onion powder*
- *1 medium onion, cut into 6 pieces*
- *1 tablespoon coarse salt*

1. Put meat in roaster. Mix the water, liquid smoke, chili powder, garlic powder, onion powder, and salt. Pour over roast. Add the onion. The meat may marinate anywhere from all day to overnight. Bring to room temperature before cooking.

2. Roast in a preheated 250° (121° C) oven 3 to 4 hours,

depending on quality and thickness of meat. Turn meat after 1½ hours. Pour off gravy near end of cooking time. Skim fat and reheat.

Carol's notes: A steak under 1-inch thick cooks in 2½ to 3 hours. Potatoes, peeled and cut into large pieces, may be added 1 hour before meat is done.

EASIEST COOKBOOK BARBECUED BEEF PARTY

CHEESE BOARD

BLACK OLIVES

SWEET PICKLES

BARBECUED BEEF ON BUNS

EASIEST COLESLAW

BEER AND WINE

HEAVENLY HASH CAKE

PARTY BARBECUED BEEF

6 to 8 servings

The beef is made in advance, then sauced the day of the do.

PREPARATION TIME: Under 30 minutes
COOKING TIME: About 4 hours
BEST UTENSILS: Roaster with lid; large skillet

1 5-pound (2.3-kg) brisket of beef
Coarse salt
Freshly ground black pepper
3 medium onions, sliced
½ cup water

For the Sauce

1 cup broth from meat
1 16-ounce (480-ml) bottle barbecue sauce
1 tablespoon vinegar
2 tablespoons Worcestershire sauce
1 teaspoon chili powder
½ teaspoon Wright's liquid smoke

1. Season the brisket with salt and pepper. Make a bed of onions in the bottom of the roaster. Lay beef on top. Add the water. Cover and roast in a preheated 325° (163° C) oven 3 to 4 hours or until it is tender throughout when tested with fork tines.

2. Let the brisket cool, then wrap well in foil and store in refrigerator. Refrigerate gravy, covered, in a bowl.

3. Slice cold beef thin, then allow it to warm to room temperature. Scrape congealed fat from gravy.

4. In a large skillet, mix and heat the meat gravy, bottled sauce, vinegar, Worcestershire sauce, chili powder, and liquid smoke. When sauce reaches the boiling point, add the beef, making sure each slice is coated with sauce. Cover skillet and cook over low heat until barbecued meat and sauce are very hot.

Carol's note: To serve, arrange beef slices and sauce in a shallow casserole kept warm on a hot tray.

Heat barbecue buns, wrapped in foil, in a 250° (121° C) oven for 20 minutes. Guests make their own sandwiches.

V. Pork

RED-ROASTED RIBS

HAM AND PORK LOAF

CRISP FRIED PORK CHOPS

BROILED MUSTARD-GLAZED PORK CHOPS

EASIEST COOKBOOK PETITE CHOUCROUTE GARNIE DINNER PARTY

PETITE CHOUCROUTE GARNIE

ROAST PORK TENDERLOIN WITH BOURBON AND SOY

HAM WITH RED GRAVY

RENI'S ROAST PORK

WURST WITH ONIONS

TED AND JO'S GLAZED BAKED HAM

HAM SALAD WITH VINEGAR DRESSING

BARBECUED SPARERIBS

I like to roam the streets of Chinatown in New York and Los Angeles. Popping in and out of the markets, surrounded by big sacks of rice and bins of gingerroot, inhaling the drying smoked ducks and red roasted, fat hunks of pork, I am in another world.

I search the shelves for canned quail eggs to serve dipped in soy sauce as an appetizer and appreciate, but pass by, the cans of boiled lotus and the omnipresent cellophane bags of tiny dried fish. One day, I promise myself, I shall learn what to do with tiny dried fish.

I do know, however, what to do with Chinese sausages that look and taste exactly the same in San Francisco, New York, London, or Port of Spain, Trinidad—as if one large factory were supplying the whole world. These red-hued slim sausages are linked in pairs and usually hang on hooks above head level. Some markets refrigerate them.

For an appetizer, slice Chinese sausages (1 for each person) into ½-inch (1.3-cm) pieces and fry them over medium-high heat for 5 minutes on each side, until they are very crisp.

Or spoon fried Chinese sausages (2 per person) and their sweet-tasting fat over steamed rice and serve with Bean Sprout Salad. Some people, including me, think Chinese food tastes better when eaten with chopsticks.

RED-ROASTED RIBS

4 servings

Red-roasting is a Chinese method of cooking, so-called because the soy sauce turns the gravy red. Use "country-style" spareribs, the small rib rack from the end of the loin. Ribs should be of a light pink-gray color, meaty and lean.

PREPARATION TIME: 15 minutes
COOKING TIME: 2½ hours
BEST UTENSIL: Roaster with lid

5 pounds (2.2 kg) country-style pork ribs
2 scallions, dewhiskered and cut into 2-inch (5-cm) pieces
3 garlic cloves, coarsely chopped
⅓ cup Japanese soy sauce
⅓ cup dry sherry
1-inch (2.5-cm) piece fresh gingerroot, chopped
1 cup water
1 teaspoon raw sugar

1. Cut away excess fat from ribs, but don't slice apart or separate ribs.

2. Put the ribs into roasting pan with the scallions, garlic, soy sauce, sherry, ginger, water, and sugar. Roast, covered, in a preheated 325° (163° C) oven for 2 hours, until meat is almost falling from bones.

HAM AND PORK LOAF

4 to 6 servings

Iced with a slightly sweet glaze that doesn't distract from or disguise ham's smoky flavor.

PREPARATION TIME: 20 minutes
COOKING TIME: 1¾ hours
BEST UTENSIL: Shallow baking pan

1 pound (454 g) ground ham
1 pound (454 g) lean ground pork
2 large eggs
1 cup bread crumbs
½ cup milk
¼ teaspoon freshly ground black pepper

For the Glaze

½ cup catsup
½ cup red wine vinegar
½ cup sugar
1 teaspoon Coleman's dry mustard

1. Combine the ham, pork, eggs, bread crumbs, milk, and pepper in a large bowl. Shape into an oval loaf and place in baking pan.

2. Wire-whisk together the catsup, vinegar, sugar, and dry mustard. Spoon evenly over the loaf.

3. Cover the loaf with aluminum foil and bake in a preheated 300° (149° C) oven for 1 hour. Uncover, spoon pan juices over top, and bake, uncovered, for 45 minutes more. Spoon pan gravy over loaf once or twice.

Carol's note: Serve with a green salad tossed with a wine vinegar and olive oil dressing.

CRISP FRIED PORK CHOPS

3 or 4 servings

PREPARATION TIME: 15 minutes
COOKING TIME: About 10 minutes
BEST UTENSIL: Large skillet

- 8 *rib or loin pork chops, sliced thin (visible and available in supermarkets)*
- 2 *large eggs*
- ½ *teaspoon coarse salt*
- 1 *cup bread crumbs*
- 1 *cup peanut oil*

1. Pat the chops dry with paper towels. Beat the eggs and salt together in a bowl large enough to dip the chops. Spread the bread crumbs on a plate.

2. Dip both sides of pork chops in the egg, then coat heavily with the bread crumbs. (Chops may be breaded in advance and stored in refrigerator. Bring to room temperature before frying.)

3. Heat the oil over medium-high heat. When the oil is very hot, add the chops and fry for 5 minutes on each side. Drain on paper towels.

Carol's note: Good with Shoepeg Corn Pudding and sliced tomatoes.

BROILED MUSTARD-GLAZED PORK CHOPS

4 servings

PREPARATION TIME: Under 10 minutes
COOKING TIME: About 20 minutes
BEST UTENSIL: Shallow pan or stove broiling tray

8 rib pork chops, cut ½ inch (1.3 cm) thick
Prepared mustard

1. Brush one side of the chops with mustard.

2. Broil 5 to 6 inches (13 to 15 cm) from the heat source for 10 minutes on the first side. Turn and baste with more mustard (fresh mustard, not the pan juices). Broil 10 more minutes, or until chops are brown and done (gray-colored throughout).

EASIEST COOKBOOK PETITE CHOUCROUTE GARNIE DINNER PARTY

PÂTÉ

PETITE CHOUCROUTE GARNIE
(GARNISHED SAUERKRAUT)

BEER or
ROSÉ WINE

BOILED POTATOES

BLACK BREAD

HUNGARIAN PEPPERS
(Jarred)

DIJON MUSTARD

EASIEST CHEESECAKE

PETITE CHOUCROUTE GARNIE

6 servings

Ten tiny juniper berries perfume the sauerkraut as it simmers in a wine-beef broth, to be served "garnished" with a lovely loin of pork.

PREPARATION TIME: Under 30 minutes
COOKING TIME: 4 hours
BEST UTENSIL: Large top-of-stove casserole

4 pounds (2 kg) boned pork loin
3 pounds (1.4 kg) fresh sauerkraut
2 strips bacon
2 medium onions, sliced thin
2 cups dry white wine
1 cup mild beef broth
1 large bay leaf
10 juniper berries
(locate the berries, bottled, on the spice rack)
10 peppercorns
1 teaspoon salt

1. Rinse the sauerkraut in a colander under cold running water to remove briny taste. Separate strands and drain well.

2. Line the casserole with the bacon strips. Make layers of the sauerkraut and onions, then add the wine, beef broth, bay leaf, juniper berries, peppercorns, and salt. Put the pork on top.

3. Bring liquid to a boil on top of the stove, then cover the casserole and bake in a preheated 300° (149° C) oven for 4 hours. Stir the kraut occasionally. Turn the meat after 2 hours.

4. Heap sauerkraut on a platter (preferably hot) and surround with the pork, neatly sliced.

ROAST PORK TENDERLOIN WITH BOURBON AND SOY

4 servings

From under the rib section. Sometimes sold tied for shape's sake. You don't have to use your good Jack Daniels for this—any bourbon will do.

PREPARATION TIME: Under 10 minutes
COOKING TIME: About 1½ hours
BEST UTENSIL: Shallow roasting pan

1 *2- to 3-pound (.9- to 1.4-kg) pork tenderloin*
½ *cup bourbon whiskey*
½ *cup Japanese soy sauce*
3 *tablespoons honey*
(I use organic "clover")

1. Combine the bourbon, soy sauce, and honey. Pour over and rub into meat. Roast may marinate several hours.

2. Roast the pork uncovered in a preheated 325° (163° C) oven for 1½ hours, or until a meat thermometer inserted into the loin registers 170° (77° C). Baste occasionally with pan juices.

Carol's notes: Serve with Easiest Rice and Bean-Sprout Salad.

A high-spirited appetizer. Slice thin, spear with toothpicks, and keep warm on a hot tray.

HAM WITH RED GRAVY

2 to 4 servings

Coffee and cream are the unexpected ingredients that color this Southern comfort red.

PREPARATION TIME: Under 10 minutes
COOKING TIME: Under 15 minutes
BEST UTENSIL: Large skillet

2 to 3 *tablespoons butter*
1 or 2 *1-pound (454-g) smoked hams slices, cut ¼ inch (6 mm) thick*
¼ to ½ *cup heavy cream*
¼ to ½ *cup hot strong coffee (Instant is OK)*

1. Melt the butter in the skillet over medium heat. When the fat is hot, fry the ham about 5 minutes on each side. Turn with tongs once or twice.

2. Remove the ham to a plate. Add the cream and coffee to skillet. To make red gravy, stir the liquid with a wire whisk until it reduces to gravy consistency (about 1 to 2 minutes). Pour over ham.

Carol's note: A casual supper or a bracing brunch could include fried eggs or grits and a seasonal fresh fruit.

RENI'S ROAST PORK

4 to 6 servings

"You take a little chopped-up onion, a lot of peppercorns, minced garlic, and some olive oil; then you mash it all up in a mortar with the pestle until the mixture is like loose paste."

That's what I did to season many a porker because that's how Reni Santoni told me to do it because that's the way his mother, Esther Rodriguez, did it, and that's the way *her* mother, Amalia Uson, did it.

One day, as I was about to do it with the onion, the peppercorns, the garlic, the olive oil, the mortar and pestle, that inspiration which comes from indolence struck, and I impetuously threw all the ingredients into the blender, whirling them into an onion-garlic paste perfect enough to please Señoras Uson and Rodriguez *and* Reni.

With black beans and steamed rice, the dinner is classic Spanish and one of my favorites.

PREPARATION TIME: 10 minutes
COOKING TIME: About 2 hours
BEST UTENSIL: Roasting pan

- 1 *8-chop center-cut pork loin roast, with bones, about 6 pounds (2.8 kg)*
  (have butcher saw in between bones to facilitate carving into separate chops for serving)
- ½ *small onion, coarsely cut*
- 3 *large garlic cloves*
- 10 *peppercorns*
- 2 *tablespoons olive oil*

1. Whirl the onion, garlic, peppercorns, and olive oil in the blender, or mash by hand in a mortar and pestle. (Food processors can't crack peppercorns.) The mixture should have the texture of loose paste.

2. Pat the roast dry. Rub entire surface of roast with

onion-garlic paste. Work some into the slashes where the backbone has been sawed.

3. Insert a meat thermometer (wherever you can, without touching the bone) and roast, uncovered, fat side up, in a preheated 325° (163° C) oven. Roast 2 hours, or until the thermometer registers 175° (79° C), well done.

WURST WITH ONIONS

4 servings

My choice is Weisswurst, but it may be done with Brat-, Bock-, or Knock-.

PREPARATION TIME: Under 15 minutes
COOKING TIME: About 30 minutes
BEST UTENSIL: Large skillet

8 *fresh sausages*
4 *medium onions, sliced thin and separated into rings*

1. Pour and spread a thin coat of oil over the bottom of a skillet. Heat oil over medium heat. When hot, fry the sausages for 10 minutes, turning often with tongs to brown evenly.

2. Add the onions to the skillet. Stir and brown with sausages for 15 more minutes.

3. Reduce heat slightly, cover the skillet, and steam for 5 minutes or until wurst are hot throughout.

Carol's notes: The recipe may be halved.

Serve with black bread and butter, a platter of sliced cucumber and/or tomatoes, hot mustard, and cold beer.

TED AND JO'S GLAZED BAKED HAM

6 to 12 servings

Teresa (Ted) Shapiro and Josephine (Jo) Caruso are indomitable cooks. This is their Christmas ham.

PREPARATION TIME: Under 30 minutes
COOKING TIME: 2½ to 4 hours (about 15 minutes per pound)
BEST UTENSIL: Large shallow baking pan and rack

1 10- to 20-pound (5- to 9-kg) smoked ham, bone in
10 to 20 cloves
1 jar prepared ham glaze
1 8-ounce (227-g) can pineapple chunks
1 jar maraschino cherries

1. Wipe off the ham with paper towels. Leave on the rind or skin. Put the ham, fat side up, on the roaster rack. Bake uncovered in a preheated 325° (163° C) oven for 1 hour.

2. Remove the ham from the oven and cut away the skin. Score ham by crisscrossing long diagonal slashes across the fat. Stud fat with the cloves.

3. Continue baking ham until 1 hour before it is done. Spread on the ham glaze, then attach the pineapple chunks and the cherries with toothpicks.

4. Bake ham for the final hour. A meat thermometer inserted halfway down into the meat will register 155° (68° C) for done. Make sure thermometer does not rest on bone.

HAM SALAD WITH VINEGAR DRESSING

PREPARATION TIME: Under 30 minutes
COOKING TIME: None
BEST UTENSIL: Large glass bowl

2 *cups leftover baked ham*
1 *Spanish onion, sliced thin*
6 *tablespoons wine vinegar*
½ *cup water*

1. Cut the ham into ½-inch (1.3-cm) cubes.

2. Combine the ham, onion, vinegar, and water. Mix well and marinate at least 2 or 3 hours.

Carol's note: Fill the hollows of avocado halves with ham salad.

BARBECUED SPARERIBS

4 servings

I'm sure I cut my teeth on these. St. Louis, my hometown, is still a Bar-B-Q town, and some folks drive miles to their favorite hickory pit.

PREPARATION TIME: 15 minutes
COOKING TIME: 2 hours
BEST UTENSIL: Large shallow baking pan

5 pounds (2.3 kg) lean pink spareribs (allow 1 pound per person, plus 1 pound extra)

Barbecue Sauce

2 cups catsup
¼ cup Worcestershire sauce
1 teaspoon chili powder
1 tablespoon vinegar
¼ teaspoon Wright's liquid smoke (the only brand I have ever seen)

1. Arrange the ribs in pan in one layer. Roast in a preheated 350° (177° C) oven for 1 hour. Pour off fat. Barbecue 1 more hour, basting every 15 minutes with the following sauce.

2. Combine the catsup, Worcestershire sauce, chili powder, vinegar, and liquid smoke in a small pot. Bring to a boil over medium heat, then simmer 5 minutes. Reheat extra sauce for the table.

Carol's note: Serve with baked potatoes in winter, fresh corn in summer, and a tossed salad with sour cream–bleu cheese dressing.

VI. Lamb

I was asked to test fifty recipes from a cookbook on French regional cooking. The book, originally published in French, was to be translated into English for American publication.

The region of France assigned to me was Alsace-Lorraine, renowned for foie gras, quiche Lorraine, Choucroute Garnie, and Riesling wine.

Armed with a French dictionary and a metric system conversion table, I started cooking.

During the time of the recipe testing, I, David, and our friends Bruce and Carole Hart spent summer weekends away from the city on 125 acres of open fields, blueberry bushes, privacy, and a swimming pond shared with perch and pike.

We were all enthusiastic at the opportunity to sample some "authentic" Alsatian dishes. The quiche Lorraine (bacon and egg custard in a pastry shell) was exclaimed over, and the Choucroute Garnie (sauerkraut garnished with pork meats) tasted terrific one raining, thundering night. (I noted in my report to the cookbook's editor that I had omitted two pounds of fresh pork fat called for in the recipe.)

The trouble came during the "weekend of the mussels."

For Friday night dinner, my main course was filet mignon, smothered with a creamy mushroom gravy. My good friends and relative politely ate some of the sauce before they scraped it off their steaks.

On Saturday, I accurately followed another Alsatian recipe's instructions and marinated fillets of pike in Madeira wine for six hours. When baked, the fish was sodden. It was like eating fillets of wine.

Usually for Sunday breakfast we looked forward to smoked whitefish and Nova Scotia salmon, but I had to test Mussels and Poached Eggs with Hollandaise Sauce, the trick being to incorporate liquid from the steamed mussels into the sauce.

The mussels were the dirtiest I'd ever cleaned, and there were fifty of them. Even with a sturdy wire brush and elbow grease, it wasn't easy to remove the rock-hard parasites from their comfortable home on each dark purple shell. Everyone took a turn scraping the mussels. I suspected a plot to desert me for town and bacon and eggs.

It took from ten in the morning until three in the afternoon to get "breakfast" on the table. The finished dish looked beautiful: tender steamed mussels circling white-sauced poached eggs. But there was general agreement that mussels and eggs do not go together. I tried not to take it personally.

Sunday night was not the time to uncover the Tripe á la mode de Caen. Flavored with calvados (apple brandy), the casserole had slow-cooked in the oven for two days.

The aroma was wonderful. I force-fed everyone spoonfuls of the rich, fat sauce and slivers of tripe before we went out for a pizza.

The following weekend, my recipe-testing assignment was completed, and I prepared one of my own Easiest recipes, Irish Stew. While the pot simmered, I read a book, relieved that my afternoons of scraping mussels and concocting complicated sauces were over.

The troops loved the stew.

The projected translation of the book on French regional cooking was never published.

EASIEST IRISH STEW

4 to 6 servings

PREPARATION TIME: 15 minutes
COOKING TIME: 2 to 2½ hours
BEST UTENSIL: Large casserole

3 pounds (1.4 kg) lean shoulder of lamb, bone in (thick chunks are preferable)
Coarse salt
Freshly ground black pepper
1 large potato, sliced thin
3 or 4 medium onions, sliced thin
2 cups water
6 medium potatoes
6 carrots, pared
1 tablespoon fresh dill, chopped

1. Pat the lamb dry. Season with salt and pepper.

2. Spread the sliced potato on the bottom of the casserole. Lightly salt and pepper. Layer on the onions, then place lamb pieces on top of onions. Add the water.

3. Cover and bake in a 325° (163° C) preheated oven for 1 hour. Then arrange the potatoes and carrots on top of the lamb. Season with salt and pepper. If liquid is low, add a little water.

4. Bake 1 to 1½ hours more, until lamb is very tender. Before serving, sprinkle the fresh dill on top.

ROAST LEG OF LAMB

6 servings

PREPARATION TIME: Under 15 minutes
COOKING TIME: About 1¼ to 1½ hours for pink or medium
BEST UTENSIL: Roaster and rack

1 6-pound (2.7-kg) leg of lamb (quality lamb is light red with white fat)
2 tablespoons olive oil, 2 tablespoons fresh lemon juice, and 2 large garlic cloves, pressed, for marinade
or
prepared Dijon mustard

1. Wipe the roast dry with paper towels. In a small bowl, mix the olive oil and lemon juice. Press in the garlic, then rub marinade into entire surface of meat. *Or,* instead of marinade, rub entire surface of meat with a light coating of mustard.

2. Insert meat thermometer halfway down into thickest part of leg. Roast the lamb uncovered, fat side up, on a rack in a preheated 325° (163° C) oven. Cook until the temperature on meat thermometer reaches 145 to 150° (63° to 66° C) for pink. Make sure thermometer does not rest on bone.

Carol's notes: A half leg may be roasted. Either the shank or the butt end will take approximately the same time as a whole leg.
For an unusual Easiest Dinner, serve with Saffron Rice and Greek Salad.

POTTED PIQUANT LEG OF LAMB

6 servings

PREPARATION TIME: 15 minutes
COOKING TIME: 3 hours
BEST UTENSIL: Large deep roaster

1 *6-pound (2.7-kg) leg of lamb*
Coarse salt
Freshly ground black pepper
Garlic powder
Gravy Master
2 *medium-sized onions, coarsely chopped*
2 *tablespoons flour*
2 *cups water*
1 *cup vinegar*
¼ *cup catsup*
2 *tablespoons sugar*
1 *tablespoon coarse salt*

1. Carefully cut off all the lamb fat you can. Season meat with salt, pepper, and garlic powder. Rub a light coat of Gravy Master over the surface of the lamb. Put the lamb in the roaster on a bed of the chopped onions.

2. Mix together the flour, water, vinegar, catsup, sugar, and the tablespoon of salt. Add to roaster.

3. Cover pan and roast lamb in a preheated 350° (177° C) oven for 3 hours, or until the lamb is nearly falling from the bone. Turn meat once or twice during cooking.

4. After 2 hours of cooking, pour off the gravy (leave some to moisten lamb) and skim the fat. Reheat the slightly sweet-sour sauce at serving time.

Carol's note: A half leg of lamb may be prepared in a smaller roaster, using the same amount of sauce ingredients.

BROILED LAMB STEAK

4 servings

Robust, large cuts from the leg of lamb are briefly broiled.

PREPARATION TIME: Under 15 minutes
COOKING TIME: Under 15 minutes
BEST UTENSIL: Oven's broiling tray

4 *lamb steaks, cut 1 inch (2.5 cm) thick*
2 *tablespoons olive oil, 2 tablespoons fresh lemon juice, ¼ teaspoon coarse salt, freshly ground black pepper, and 2 garlic cloves, pressed, for marinade*
or
Gravy Master

1. Combine olive oil, lemon juice, salt, pepper, and garlic and rub into both sides of steaks. Marinate anywhere from 1 to 2 hours up to overnight in the refrigerator. *Or,* instead of marinade, lightly brush the steaks with Gravy Master.

2. Broil in a preheated broiler 5 to 6 minutes on each side. Steaks should be 3 to 4 inches (8 to 10 cm) from the heat.

Carol's note: I tested this recipe in my electric stove in L.A. and my gas stove in N.Y. The timing was approximately the same.

LAMB STEAKS WITH ANCHOVY SAUCE

2 to 4 servings

PREPARATION TIME: 15 minutes
COOKING TIME: Under 10 minutes
BEST UTENSIL: 1 or 2 large skillets

4 to 8 lamb steaks from the shank end, sliced thin, about ¼ inch (6 mm) thick
Coarse salt
Olive oil
2 teaspoons anchovy paste
4 ounces (113 g) sweet butter (1 stick), softened

1. Flatten the lamb steaks with a meat mallet or the bottom of a coffee mug, taking care not to split the skin. Salt lightly. Combine anchovy paste and butter.

2. Cover the bottom of the skillet(s) with olive oil. Place over medium-high heat. When a drop of water spatters in the pan, add the steaks and sauté them for 1 minute on each side, until they are browned. Turn with tongs. Lower the heat and cook 3 to 4 minutes more, or until a test cut near the bone is properly pink.

3. Remove the cooked steaks to a platter. Work quickly. Add the anchovy butter to the pan(s). Use low heat to whisk into pan juices. Spoon hot sauce over lamb steaks.

CALDERADA

4 servings

A calderada is a Spanish pot or casserole. This calderada is filled with lamb, lemon, and wine.

PREPARATION TIME: 15 minutes
COOKING TIME: 1½ to 2 hours
BEST UTENSIL: Large casserole

3 to 5 pounds (1.4 to 2.3 kg) lean lamb with bone (shoulder steaks, finest quality neck, or extra lean "riblets" may be used)
Coarse salt
Freshly ground black pepper
3 medium onions, thinly sliced
1 lemon, thinly sliced
3 or 4 cloves garlic, sliced or coarsely chopped
Bay leaf
1 cup dry white wine
1 cup water
¼ cup olive oil

1. Salt and pepper the meat. If using shoulder or neck, cut into small cubes or pieces. If using riblets, separate.

2. Layer the onions, lamb, and lemon in the casserole. Strew with garlic. Add the bay leaf, wine, water, and olive oil.

3. Bake, covered, in a preheated 300° (149° C) oven for 1½ to 2 hours, or until lamb is very tender.

BAKED LAMB AND LENTILS

4 servings

PREPARATION TIME: Under 30 minutes
COOKING TIME: About 2 hours
BEST UTENSIL: Medium-sized deep casserole with lid

- 2 *pounds (.9 kg) lean, boneless lamb shoulder cut into 1-inch (2.5-cm) cubes*
- 1 *cup lentils*
- 1 *medium onion, sliced thin*
- 2 *garlic cloves, sliced thin*
- 2 *ribs celery, sliced thin*
- 2 *carrots, sliced thin*
- 1 *bay leaf*
- ½ *teaspoon coarse salt*
- ¼ *teaspoon freshly ground black pepper*
- 1 *cup dry red wine*
- 1 *teaspoon dry mustard mixed with 1 cup water*

1. Trim the lamb of excess fat. Rinse the lentils in a strainer under cold running water.

2. Put the lentils into the casserole with the onion, garlic, celery, carrots, bay leaf, salt, pepper, wine, and mustard-water mixture. Arrange the lamb on top.

3. Bake, covered, in a preheated 350° (177° C) oven for 1 hour. Stir. Liquid should barely simmer. Reduce oven heat if necessary. Recover and bake 1 hour more, or until lentils are very soft and lamb is fork tender.

Carol's note: This recipe may be halved. Use a 2-quart (1.9-l) small casserole.

BROILED LAMB CHOPS, THREE WAYS

4 servings

On cue, when asked if there is anything "different" to do with lamb chops, I give out Gene Gabriel's Lamb Chops Basted with Pomegranate Juice. Gene, a retired thespian, claims he learned the recipe traveling with a troupe of Armenian acrobats.

PREPARATION TIME: 10 minutes
COOKING TIME: About 10 minutes
BEST UTENSIL: Stove's broiling tray, with rack (line bottom with foil to collect lamb fat)

8 lean rib or loin lamb chops, cut ¾ inch (1.9 cm) thick
Gravy concentrate
or
Olive oil, fresh lemon juice, pressed garlic, coarse salt, freshly ground black pepper, to taste
or
1 cup fresh pomegranate juice (bottled and sold in "health food" stores and some supermarkets)

1. Pat the chops dry. Trim excess fat from chops, leaving a small border. Slash border in two or three places to prevent chops from curling while cooking.

2. If using gravy concentrate, lightly brush both sides of chops. *Or* mix together olive oil, lemon juice, garlic, salt, and pepper and coat the chops, which may marinate 1 to 2 hours. *Or* baste both sides of meat with the pomegranate juice.

3. Broil chops in a preheated broiler 3 to 4 inches from the heat for 5 to 6 minutes on the first side. If using the pomegranate juice, baste before and after turning.

4. Broil 7 to 8 minutes on the second side for a slightly pink chop. Cut near bone to check for doneness.

LAMB IN RED WINE

4 servings

PREPARATION TIME: 15 minutes
COOKING TIME: 2 to 2½ hours
BEST UTENSIL: Medium top-of-stove casserole

2 pounds (.9 kg) lean lamb shoulder, boned or 3 pounds (1.4 kg) with bone
2 tablespoons flour
Dry red wine to cover, about 4 cups
4 carrots, pared and chuncked
2 medium onions, each cut into 8 pieces
2 tablespoons salt
10 peppercorns
1 teaspoon sugar

1. Put the lamb in the casserole. Mix the flour with ½ cup of the wine. Pour over the meat with the rest of the wine. Add the carrots, onions, salt, peppercorns, and sugar.

2. Bring the liquid to a boil on top of the stove, then bake, covered, in a preheated 325° (163° C) oven for 2 to 2½ hours, or until the lamb is very tender. Skim off any fat.

Carol's notes: To divide recipe, use a small 2-quart (1.9-l) casserole.

May be made the day before. Reheat slowly.

Serve with Greek Salad and pita bread.

EASIEST COOKBOOK CURRY PARTY

WHOLE SMOKED WHITEFISH
or
SMOKED OYSTERS ON TOOTHPICKS
CHERRY TOMATOES
LAMB KIMA CURRY
SAFFRON RICE WITH RAISINS AND ALMONDS
MANGO CHUTNEY
MINCED ONIONS
CUCUMBERS IN YOGURT
FRESH FRUIT
ICED CREAM

LAMB KIMA CURRY

6 servings

An unusual curry, but mild. Company-safe.

PREPARATION TIME: Under 30 minutes
COOKING TIME: About 1¼ hours
BEST UTENSIL: Large top-of-stove casserole

3 to 3½ pounds (1.4 to 1.6 kg) lean ground shoulder of lamb
(ask butcher to trim fat before grinding)
3 medium onions, chopped
(about 3 cups frozen chopped onions acceptable)
4 teaspoons ground turmeric
2 teaspoons ground coriander
1 teaspoon ground cumin
1 tablespoon crushed red pepper
1 16-ounce (454-g) can peeled whole tomatoes
1 tablespoon salt
1 9-ounce (255-g) package frozen peas
(defrost for 15 to 20 minutes)

1. Put the lamb and onions in the casserole. Brown lamb over medium heat until all red is gone from meat. Stir frequently. Break up lamb into small pieces with a large spoon.

2. Combine the turmeric, coriander, cumin, and red pepper. Add the spices, stirring in so that the lamb and onions are coated.

3. Add the tomatoes, breaking them up with the edge of a large spoon. Then add the salt. Stir. Cover the casserole, reduce heat to low, and simmer for approximately 1¼ hours. Spoon off any fat that has risen to surface. (If cooked the day before, fat will harden in refrigerator and lift off easily.)

4. Add the peas 15 to 20 minutes before serving time. (Adding them at the last minute keeps them crisp and unwrinkled.) The curry is finished when the meat and peas are steaming hot.

VII. Side Dishes

SANGRIA
ARTICHOKES WITH GARLIC AND PARSLEY
ASPARAGUS TIPS WITH PARMESAN CHEESE
SAUTÉED BEAN SPROUTS
BEAN-SPROUT SALAD
BARB'S BEER BREAD
HORN AND HARDART'S BAKED BEANS
SEÑOR SILVA SILVA'S BLACK BEAN SOUP
SMOKY CHILI BEANS
GLENN'S COLD BEET BORSCHT
EASIEST COLESLAW
SMOTHERED CABBAGE
BESS'S CHINESE CABBAGE
HOMEMADE CRANBERRY SAUCE
CORN-ON-THE-COB
SHOEPEG CORN PUDDING
CUCUMBER SALAD
CUCUMBERS IN YOGURT
HOMEMADE PICKLES
GREEK SALAD
ENDIVE SALAD
SALADE NIÇOISE
SNAP BEANS, SOUTHERN STYLE
MUSHROOMS IN SOY
OVEN-ROASTED ONIONS
MACARONI AND CHEESE CUSTARD

TURK'S NOODLES WITH COTTAGE CHEESE

PASTA

GARLIC AND OIL SAUCE

EASIEST TOMATO SAUCE

PESTO

BAKED SWEET POTATOES

SAFFRON POTATOES

ESTHER'S SWEET POTATO PIE

BAKED POTATOES

ANN'S POTATOES ANNA

BOILED OR OVEN-BROWNED POTATOES

EASIEST RICE

SAFFRON RICE WITH RAISINS AND ALMONDS

SAUTÉED FRESH SPINACH

ACORN SQUASH

BUTTER-BAKED ZUCCHINI IN FOIL

SAUERKRAUT IN BEER

WATERCRESS AND SCALLION SALAD

I was invited to a large cocktail buffet dinner party. The main course for the evening, loudly and repeatedly announced to all arriving, was Carol Guilford's Bouillabaisse (Provençal fish and shellfish in a saffron soup), stewed without deviation from her (my) recipe in *Carol Guilford's Main Course Cookbook.*

Swiftly, I calculated all that could go wrong with the recipe. Would the clams be tough, the fish dry, the saffron missing? No. Tender clams, moist fish with the unmistakable yellow color and taste of saffron threads.

My recipe reads, "Ladle the Bouillabaisse into deep bowls." This Bouillabaisse was spooned onto flat plates. You can't put soup on plates. "Delicious," one man told me, "absolutely delicious," as I watched the beautiful broth slide off his plate and onto the rug.

At a formal sit-down dinner, I and other guests were given Hungarian stuffed cabbage as a first course and Mexican tacos as a second course, not a complementary combination of cuisines.

There may be no help for the party-giver who pointedly asked if my husband and I liked seafood and then served us Tuna Noodle Casserole.

Generosity and sensitivity are the keys to gracious entertaining. One hostess at a seven-to-nine cocktail party locked the liquor cabinet punctually at nine. The remains of a ripe, runny Brie and a mediocre pâté were wheeled out by a uniformed person. Then the lights blinked off and on. Feeling as if the junior prom had come to an abrupt end, three of us adjourned to the garden and lustily sang a chorus of "The Party's Over."

One New Year's Eve when I was working in a Broadway musical, the entire cast was invited to our star's bash, to be held in the theater's downstairs lounge. We were allowed one guest, and those who were attending were asked to sign their names to a sheet thumbtacked to the bulletin board. We were all excited.

The party turned out to be an hour of bad champagne, hot dogs, and no music. That's life on the wicked stage.

The best party I ever gave—not counting the one at

Antonio's Restaurant in Los Angeles with margaritas, mariachis, and Mexican mole—was on July 4, 1976.

New York City shivered with Bicentennial enthusiasm. Everyone with a sliver of river view including me, gave parties for their friends to see the old sailing vessels called the Tall Ships sail and parade up the Hudson River.

For eye-openers there were Bloody Marys, Screwdrivers, white wine, and champagne. On the buffet table, dishes in a revolving silver lazy Susan were filled with marinated mushrooms, eggplant, chick-peas, olives, cucumber strips, and artichoke hearts. There was a combination cheese board, pâté and sweet gherkins, and a large platter of deviled eggs.

For the main attraction of my Independence Day Menu, I chose that holiday's traditional Whole Poached Salmon with Homemade Mayonnaise. When the fish was arranged on its long wooden board, decorated with cress and lemon, it looked "catered," as one guest put it, but I was intrigued by the fish's color, the hue true "salmon-pink." I patted myself on the back for having measured the poacher and board before I bought the fish.

For the rest of the patriotic brunch, there were fried chicken wings that stayed hot and crisp on an electric hot tray and a salad of bean sprouts, selected for their long-lasting crunch.

A large crystal bowl held big red-black Bing cherries and the chocolate cake bought from the Café Geiger, a German restaurant and bakery on Manhattan's East Side.

To drink, there was Sangria, Spanish red wine punch. I quintupled the recipe, filling the soup kettle and every pitcher and vase in the house. We had to run lukewarm water in the bathtub for all the bouquets of summer flowers brought by thoughtful friends.

SANGRIA

4 servings

PREPARATION TIME: 15 minutes
COOKING TIME: None
BEST UTENSIL: 2-quart (1.9-l) pitcher

2 *bottles dry red Spanish wine*
½ *cup brandy*
2 *7-ounce (207-ml) bottles club soda*
Juice of 2 small lemons
4 *tablespoons sugar*

1. Stir together the wine, brandy, club soda, lemon juice, and sugar in the pitcher. Refrigerate for at least 1 hour.

Carol's note: Thinly sliced orange slices may be added to flavor and decorate the punch.

ARTICHOKES WITH GARLIC AND PARSLEY

My favorite thistle—ten calories, five carbohydrates. Eat hot as a side dish with melted lemon butter, or cold as an appetizer or salad, dunked into vinegar and oil dressing.

PREPARATION TIME: Under 30 minutes
COOKING TIME: 45 minutes
BEST UTENSIL: Deep top-of-stove casserole with lid

4 *artichokes*
(look for fresh, green-colored closed leaves and crispiness)
4 *large garlic cloves*
½ *cup Italian or regular parsley, chopped (leafy part only)*
½ *teaspoon salt*
Olive oil
4 *thin lemon slices*

1. Wash the artichokes. Slice off the thorny tip and end of stem with a sturdy knife. Rub the cuts with lemon to prevent darkening. Snip off the lower thorn tips with kitchen scissors.

To separate the leaves, hold stem side up and whack the top side of the artichoke on a counter top. (This advice came from a viewer who had seen me on television, demonstrating how to gently pull open the leaves.)

2. Whirl the garlic and parsley in a blender or a food processor. Mix with the salt. Stuff mixture between artichoke's leaves, distributing as evenly as possible.

3. Stand artichokes upright in the casserole. Drizzle olive oil over each artichoke, then place a lemon slice on top.

4. Fill the bottom of the casserole with 2 inches (5 cm) water. Bring water to a boil, cover casserole, lower the heat, and gently boil for 40 to 45 minutes, or until a leaf easily pulls away from stem.

Carol's notes: To eat an artichoke, pull off the leaves one at a time. Dip the meaty base of the leaf into melted butter or vinegar and oil, then scrape through your teeth.
Cut away the fuzzy choke with a knife and eat artichoke bottom with a fork.
Special artichoke plates are divided to hold artichoke in center surrounded by a well for sauce and by a section for eaten leaves.

ASPARAGUS TIPS WITH PARMESAN CHEESE

For the height of spring and luxury.

PREPARATION TIME: About 10 minutes
COOKING TIME: Under 10 minutes
BEST UTENSIL: Small saucepan with lid

41 thin stalks asparagus
(look for purple, well developed, tightly closed buds; choose loose rather than prebunched stalks)
2 cups water
1 teaspoon salt
1 tablespoon butter
1 tablespoon grated Parmesan cheese

1. Slice off asparagus stalks 1 inch (2.5 cm) below tip. Wash tips well or soak in cold water 5 minutes.

2. Bring the water and salt to a boil. Add the asparagus and cook, uncovered, over medium heat for 6 to 10 minutes or until the forty-first tip tastes tender.

3. Drain quickly in a strainer, return to pot, add the butter, and cover until the butter melts. Very low heat may be used to keep tips warm. Sprinkle on the grated cheese and serve.

SAUTÉED BEAN SPROUTS

2 or 3 servings

The sprout from the tiny oriental mung bean is crunchy, healthful (it contains vitamins A, B, and C, plus calcium and iron), and fast-cooking.

PREPARATION TIME: 5 minutes
COOKING TIME: About 5 minutes
BEST UTENSIL: Large skillet

1 pound (454 g) bean sprouts
2 or 3 tablespoons peanut or soy oil
¼ cup Japanese soy sauce
4 scallions, including green part, sliced into 1-inch (2.5-cm) pieces

1. Put the bean sprouts into a colander and rinse quickly under cold running water.

2. Heat the oil in the skillet over medium-high heat. When oil is hot, add the bean sprouts and stir-fry for 3 to 4 minutes.

3. Stir in the soy sauce and scallions. Reduce heat to medium-low, cover the pan, and steam for 1 more minute. Don't overcook, as bean sprouts are 90 percent water and shrink accordingly.

Carol's note: For a main course for 2 to 4, arrange individually portioned fish fillets on top of the sprouts just before covering and steaming for the final minute. Fish is done when it is opaque. Taste-test to make sure.

BEAN-SPROUT SALAD

4 servings

PREPARATION TIME: 5 minutes
COOKING TIME: None

1½ pounds (681 g) fresh bean sprouts
¼ cup olive oil
¼ cup vinegar
1 tablespoon Japanese soy sauce
6 scallions, dewhiskered and sliced into ¼-inch (6-mm) pieces

1. Rinse the bean sprouts in a colander under cold running water.

2. Mix the sprouts with the oil, vinegar, soy sauce, and scallions. Allow flavors to meld for at least 30 minutes.

Carol's note: A very good salad for a buffet table because the sprouts stay crisp.

BARB'S BEER BREAD

My cousin Barb told me her son, Andy, has been baking "easiest homemade bread" since he was seven.

PREPARATION TIME: Under 10 minutes
COOKING TIME: 1 hour
BEST UTENSIL: Glass loaf pan

12 ounces (355 ml) bottled or canned beer
3 cups self-rising flour
3 tablespoons sugar
2 ounces (57 g) melted butter (½ stick)

1. Mix together the beer, flour, and sugar.
2. Put into a well-buttered glass loaf pan.
3. Bake in a preheated 325° (163° C) oven for 50 minutes. Pour the melted butter over the bread. Bake 10 minutes more.

Carol's note: Vary the recipe by adding chopped onion or fresh dill to the dough.

HORN AND HARDART'S BAKED BEANS

6 servings

The bygone Horn and Hardart automat on West 57th Street in New York City is unforgettable.

On cold winter days, the clattering cafeteria housed an all-walks-of-life clientele, some of whom stayed all day around the large communal tables, sipping coffee and keeping warm.

The automatic part of Horn and Hardart looked like a wall of post office boxes, but instead of mail, cooked food waited, stacked and shelved behind glass-windowed warming compartments.

As the correct change dropped into a slot, a small door automatically unlocked for the customer to lift out the selected dish.

Horn and Hardart's beans were well known for their excellence. The automatic door swung open on small brown crockery pots filled with beans, baked New England style, with their sharp smell of molasses.

I felt lucky when my portion had a sliver of crisp bacon.

The Easiest Cookbook proudly presents the authentic recipe for Horn and Hardart's baked beans.

PREPARATION TIME: Under 30 minutes
COOKING TIME: 4 hours
BEST UTENSIL: Small deep top-of-stove casserole

½ *pound (227 g) small white pea beans*
1 *small onion, chopped (½ cup)*
2 *strips raw bacon, diced*
1 *tablespoon sugar*
1½ *teaspoons salt*
1½ *tablespoons dry mustard (Coleman's)*
¼ *teaspoon red cayenne pepper*
⅓ *cup molasses*
1 *tablespoon cider vinegar*
¾ *cup tomato juice*
1 *cup water*

1. Rinse the beans well in a strainer. Put the beans into casserole and cover with water. Bring water to a boil, then reduce heat to low and simmer, covered, for 45 minutes. Drain.

2. Return the beans to casserole with the onion, bacon, sugar, salt, mustard, pepper, molasses, vinegar, tomato juice, and water. Mix well.

3. Bake, uncovered, at 250° (121° C) for 4 hours. Stir after 2 hours. If beans look dry, add a small amount of boiling water. The result is a crisp crust over gravy-bathed beans.

Carol's notes: The recipe may be doubled.

To reheat beans, add a little water, cover, and use very low heat, stirring occasionally.

SEÑOR SILVA SILVA'S BLACK BEAN SOUP

Señor Pedro Silva Silva was head chef of our vacation hotel's dining room in San Juan, Puerto Rico. He printed this treasure for me and left it in my mailbox, addressed to Best Guest.

PREPARATION TIME: Under 30 minutes
COOKING TIME: 3 hours
BEST UTENSIL: Soup kettle

16 ounces (454 g) dried black turtle beans (loose beans in bins are usually more tender and of higher quality than those in packages)
16 cups (4 quarts, almost 4 liters) water
1 bay leaf
1 large onion, chopped
2 large garlic cloves, chopped
1 teaspoon chicken base
The following herbs (listed in Señor Silva's words; use under 1/8 teaspoon):
1 touch rosemary seed
1 touch thyme leaf
1 touch oregano leaf
4 tablespoons olive oil
4 tablespoons sherry wine
About 2 tablespoons salt
Pepper, as you like

1. Wash the beans well by putting them into a large strainer and running cold water over them.

2. Put the beans in soup kettle with the water, bay leaf, onion, and garlic. Bring the liquid to a boil, then cover and gently boil the beans over low heat for 3 hours, or until they are tender.

3. Add the chicken base, rosemary, thyme, oregano, olive oil, sherry, salt, and pepper. Simmer, uncovered, until soup is reduced to 8 cups (2 liters). Cool and refrigerate. Best eaten the next day.

Carol's notes: Serve with chopped sweet onion and sour cream.

A tossed green salad and rich black bean soup make a meal.

Doubles as a side dish.

SMOKY CHILI BEANS

6 servings

Warning: hot stuff. For us who love it and can take it.

PREPARATION TIME: 15 minutes
COOKING TIME: 2½ hours
BEST UTENSIL: Medium top-of-stove casserole or saucepot

1 *cup (227 g) pinto, pink, or small red beans*
4 *cups water*
1 *medium onion, chopped*
2 *large cloves garlic, chopped*
1 *slice lemon*
1 *tablespoon chili powder*
¼ *teaspoon cumin seed*
½ *teaspoon Wright's liquid smoke*
2 *teaspoons salt*

1. Wash the beans well in a strainer or a sieve. Put them into the pot with the water, onion, garlic, lemon, chili powder, cumin seed, and liquid smoke.

2. Bring the liquid to a boil, then reduce heat to low, cover pot, and simmer for 2 hours or until the beans taste tender. Stir every 30 minutes. Add the salt after 1½ hours.

Carol's note: The recipe may be doubled. For Jalapeño Beans, add 1 sliced (jarred or canned) jalapeño pepper to the pot.

GLENN'S COLD BEET BORSCHT

4 main-course servings;
6 appetizer servings

Since Glenn Jordan and I met, a lot of borscht has gone under the bridge.

PREPARATION TIME: 10 minutes
COOKING TIME: 20 minutes
BEST UTENSIL: Bottom of a double boiler or an enamel or porcelain pot (don't use metal)

1 16-ounce (454-g) can diced beets, with their liquid
⅓ cup fresh lemon juice
2 cups tomato juice
2 cups water
1 tablespoon salt
1 teaspoon sugar
3 large eggs
Sour cream

1. Pour the beet juice from the can into the saucepan, then chop up the beets on a cutting board into even smaller pieces. No heat is used until Step 4.

2. Add the beets to the pan with the lemon juice, tomato juice, water, salt, and sugar. Stir.

3. Beat the eggs well in a small bowl, then slowly add them to the saucepan, stirring constantly with a wooden spoon.

4. Bring the soup slowly to a boil over medium-low heat, stirring constantly, for 15 to 20 minutes. The constant stirring prevents the egg from cooking. Small pieces of egg that harden may be spooned out later. Turn off the heat as soon as the boiling point is reached (bubbles form around the liquid's edge). Cool, then refrigerate. Serve cold.

Carol's note: Serve with boiled new potatoes, scallions, and sliced cucumbers.

EASIEST COLESLAW

4 servings

The ancient Romans believed cabbage to be the best remedy for drunkenness. Cato the Elder, in *De agri cultura (On Farming),* advises eating as much cabbage as possible before and after a feast, preferably cold, with vinegar.

PREPARATION TIME: 15 to 20 minutes
COOKING TIME: None

- ½ *cup mayonnaise*
- 6 *tablespoons milk*
- ½ *teaspoon salt*
- ⅛ *teaspoon dry mustard*
- 3 *tablespoons vinegar*
- ¼ *cup sweet onion, finely chopped*
- 4 *cups shredded cabbage*
  (shred cabbage by cutting it in half, then slicing down along the cut side; or shred in a food processor)

1. Combine the mayonnaise, milk, salt, mustard, vinegar, and onion with a whisk.

2. Add the cabbage, mixing well to coat all shreds. Cover and refrigerate at least 1 hour.

Carol's note: Recipe may be multiplied.

SMOTHERED CABBAGE

4 servings

PREPARATION TIME: 10 minutes
COOKING TIME: Under 10 minutes
BEST UTENSIL: Large skillet

1 medium-sized head cabbage (approximately 8 cups, shredded)
4 ounces (113 g) butter (1 stick)
Coarse salt
Freshly ground black pepper

1. Wash the cabbage. Remove wilted outer leaves, then cut out core. Shred by cutting head in half, then slicing thin down along the cut side; or shred in a food processor.

2. Melt the butter in skiller over low heat. Add the cabbage. Stir to coat well. Cover and steam 10 minutes or until cabbage is tender but still crisp. Stir once or twice. Season freely with salt and freshly ground pepper.

BESS'S CHINESE CABBAGE

Mrs. Goldberg's Bok Choy.

PREPARATION TIME: Under 15 minutes
COOKING TIME: About 15 minutes
BEST UTENSIL: Large skillet

- 2 *stalks Chinese cabbage (bok choy)*
- 2 *tablespoons peanut or soybean oil*
- 1 *tablespoon salt*
- ¼ *teaspoon garlic powder, or to taste*
- 1 *package frozen chopped spinach, almost defrosted*
- 1 *2-ounce (57-g) jar pimiento, diced (optional)*

1. Pull off outer, bruised leaves, then soak the cabbage in cold water for ½ hour.

2. Slice the cabbage crosswise in approximately 1-inch (2.5-cm) slices.

3. Put the cabbage, oil, salt, and garlic powder into the skillet. Cover and steam over medium-low heat for 5 minutes.

4. Add the spinach, re-cover, and heat for 10 minutes more, or until spinach is very hot. Cabbage should stay crisp. Add more salt. Stir in the pimiento for color, if desired.

HOMEMADE CRANBERRY SAUCE

4 to 6 servings

First-rate with all fowl.

PREPARATION TIME: Under 10 minutes
COOKING TIME: About 10 minutes
BEST UTENSIL: Medium-sized saucepot

1 cup sugar
1 cup water
2 cups fresh whole cranberries
(available fall and winter; raw berries may be frozen)
Squirt of lemon

1. Bring the sugar and water to a boil. Add the cranberries and lemon. Lower heat and gently boil, uncovered, for 10 minutes, or until skins have popped and a tested cranberry tastes tender.

2. Cool and chill.

CORN-ON-THE-COB

1 to 8 servings

"Lookee here," a farmer's boy called to me, and I, from my grandfather's yard, ran wild through the open field to see an Illinois treasure. A stalk twice as tall as I had sprung from the ground, and on it were two full fat ears of corn, the light green husks hot to touch from the August sun.

"Come on, my mom'll fix 'em up fer us."

I remember that kitchen, clean and bare, and a woman who smiled instead of talked. I can see her proficient, strong, slim fingers pulling back the corn husks and my first sight of shockingly bright yellow kernels underneath. A pot of water bubbled on the stove.

I sat on a slat-backed wooden chair. The boy brought me the cooked corn. As I lifted it from the plate, the cob dripped with butter, and when I bit in, the kernels burst with milky juice. The boy showed me how to gnaw down the rows evenly, and I tried to imitate him.

Before I left, the woman wiped my buttery, salty face with a wet cloth.

I knew I wasn't supposed to talk to strangers, much less enter an unknown house.

I've never told anyone about eating my first ear of corn-on-the-cob.

PREPARATION TIME: 10 minutes
COOKING TIME: About 5 minutes, plus time for water to boil
BEST UTENSIL: Large kettle

Water
1 *tablespoon sugar*
1 to 8 *ears of corn*
(look for corn still in the husk with dark brown silk at the end; kernels should be full and milky)

1. Fill kettle with water. Add the sugar and bring to a full rolling boil.

2. Add the corn. Cook for 5 minutes. Test a kernel with a fork tine. Remove the corn with tongs. Serve with sweet butter, coarse salt, and freshly ground black pepper at the table.

Carol's note: Keep extra ears of corn hot at the table by covering them with a cloth napkin.

SHOEPEG CORN PUDDING

6 servings

PREPARATION TIME: 15 minutes
COOKING TIME: About 45 minutes
BEST UTENSIL: 1- to 1½-quart shallow glass casserole dish

- *4 cups canned shoepeg corn, with liquid (I use 2 12-ounce [340-g] cans)*
- *2 cups milk*
- *4 eggs*
- *1 teaspoon coarse salt*
- *¼ teaspoon freshly ground black pepper*
- *1½ teaspoons sugar*
- *2 tablespoons butter*

1. Put the corn with its liquid into a glass casserole dish that has been greased with butter.

2. Whirl the eggs, milk, salt, pepper, and sugar in a blender, or mix in a bowl with rotary beater, wire whisk, or fork.

3. Pour egg-milk combination over corn. Dot with the butter.

4. Bake in a preheated 325° (163° C) oven for 45 minutes or until a knife inserted in center comes out clean.

Carol's note: The recipe may be halved.

CUCUMBER SALAD

4 servings

PREPARATION TIME: Under 15 minutes
COOKING TIME: None

2 *large cucumbers, peeled*
3 *tablespoons white vinegar*
3 *tablespoons olive oil*
¼ *teaspoon sugar*
1 *teaspoon coarse salt*

1. Slice the cucumbers thin.
2. Mix the cucumbers with the vinegar, oil, sugar, and salt. Chill for at least 1 hour.

CUCUMBERS IN YOGURT

6 servings

PREPARATION TIME: 20 minutes
COOKING TIME: None

6 *large cucumbers, peeled*
½ *tablespoon salt*
½ *pint (227 g) plain yogurt*

1. Slice the cucumbers in half lengthwise, then scoop out the seeds with a teaspoon.
2. Cut the cucumber into small cubes. Put the cubes into a bowl and mix them with the salt. Let them stand 30 minutes, then drain liquid from bowl.
3. Mix in the yogurt. Salt to taste. Refrigerate at least 2 hours.

HOMEMADE PICKLES

Makes 1 quart

Kirbys are the variety of pickling cucumber most commonly found in the markets.

PREPARATION TIME: 15 minutes
COOKING TIME: None
BEST UTENSIL: 1-quart (946-ml) food jar

4 to 6 pickling cucumbers
2 tablespoons pickling spice (a combination of cinnamon, bay leaves, mustard seed, dill seed, fenugreek, allspice, chilies, ginger, cloves, and mace—bottled commercially)
¼ cup vinegar
1 tablespoon salt
2 cloves garlic, peeled and coarsely chopped
Crushed cayenne pepper to taste for "hot" pickles

1. Wash and dry the cucumbers. Slice each cucumber into quarters.

2. Put the pickling spice, vinegar, salt, and cayenne pepper into jar. Arrange the cucumbers in jar. Add the garlic and fill the jar with water. Screw lid tightly on jar.

3. Leave cucumbers at room temperature for 3 days. (Turn jar upside down for the second day.) After third day, refrigerate.

Carol's note: Pickles will keep 2 to 3 weeks.

GREEK SALAD

**2 main-course servings;
4 appetizer or side-dish servings**

PREPARATION TIME: Under 30 minutes
COOKING TIME: None

1 *small head iceberg lettuce*
1 *small cucumber, peeled, seeded, and diced*
1 *tomato, cut into wedges*
½ *cup sweet onion, chopped*
½ *green pepper, diced*
⅛ *teaspoon dried oregano*
½ *pound (227 g) Greek feta cheese*
8 *black Greek olives*

For the Dressing

½ *cup olive oil*
¼ *cup red wine vinegar*
1 *teaspoon coarse salt*
¼ *teaspoon freshly ground black pepper*
Pinch dry mustard

1. Wash the lettuce. Dry in salad spinner or wrap in paper towels to dry.

2. Combine the dressing ingredients in a bowl and mix with a wire whisk, or shake in a screw-top jar. Set aside.

3. Put the lettuce into a deep salad bowl. Top with the cucumber, tomato, onion, and green pepper. Sprinkle on the oregano. Crumble the feta cheese over all. Add the olives. Toss salad with dressing just before serving.

ENDIVE SALAD

6 servings

PREPARATION TIME: 15 minutes
COOKING TIME: none

6 *medium heads endive*
½ *cup red wine vinegar*
⅔ *cup olive oil*
½ *tablespoon salt*
16 *to* 20 *twists of the pepper mill*
1½ *teaspoons dry mustard*
6 *drops angostura bitters*

1. Wash and dry the endive, then cut off the base from the bottom of each head and sliver vertically.

2. Combine the vinegar, olive oil, salt, pepper, mustard, and bitters in a screw-top jar. Shake briskly just before tossing with the endive.

Carol's note: For an extra rich dressing, add 1 egg yolk and 2 coarsely chopped scallions to the ingredients.

SALADE NIÇOISE

2 main servings;
4 side servings

I now own a salad spinner, which whirls salad greens dry in seconds. No more wrapping wet lettuce leaves in paper towels for me.

PREPARATION TIME: 30 minutes
COOKING TIME: None

2 small heads Boston lettuce
1 7-ounce (199-g) can solid-pack tuna, in olive oil or water (drain water-packed or vegetable-oil-packed tuna)
1 small green bell pepper, slivered
Sweet onion rings to taste
10 to 12 black olives
1 2-ounce (57-g) tin flat anchovies, drained
Vinegar and oil dressing

1. Wash and dry the lettuce leaves, discarding the outer, bruised leaves.

2. Arrange the lettuce leaves in a deep salad bowl. Add the tuna, green pepper, onion, olives, and anchovies.

3. Toss with your favorite vinegar and oil dressing just before serving.

SNAP BEANS, SOUTHERN STYLE

4 servings

Sometimes called Greasy Beans.

PREPARATION TIME: 15 to 20 minutes
COOKING TIME: 1½ hours
BEST UTENSIL: Medium-sized saucepan

2 pounds (.9 kg) fresh green (string) beans
1 or 2 smoked ham hocks
(2 hocks makes the dish a main course for 2)
1 medium onion, coarsely chopped
1 teaspoon sugar
Crushed red pepper to taste (¼ teaspoon is hot)
3½ cups water

1. Rinse the beans well, then slice or snap off end tips.

2. Put the beans in pot with the ham hock(s), onion, sugar, pepper, and water. Bring to a boil, then cover the pot, turn down heat to low, and simmer for 1 hour.

3. Uncover the pot and turn the heat up to medium. Gently boil for 20 minutes, enough time for the liquid to reduce to "pot liquor" served over the beans.

MUSHROOMS IN SOY

2 or 3 servings

Works, too, as a quick sauce for meat, fish, chicken, or vegetables.

PREPARATION TIME: 10 minutes
COOKING TIME: 15 to 20 minutes
BEST UTENSIL: Aluminum foil

½ *pound (227 g) fresh mushrooms*
⅓ *cup Japanese soy sauce (approximately)*

1. Wash the mushrooms under cold running water. Cut off tough stem end, then slice diagonally through cap and stem.

2. Put the mushrooms on an ample sheet of foil. Pour the soy sauce over them. Fold package style. Bake in a 325° to 350° (163° to 177° C) oven 20 to 25 minutes.

OVEN-ROASTED ONIONS

4 to 6 servings

Luther Burbank, the American plant breeder, developed a "tearless" onion, ultimately rejected by the consumer because when it was cooked it had no smell and failed to fill the air with the onion bulb's unique and pleasant odor.

PREPARATION TIME: 5 minutes
COOKING TIME: 1 hour
BEST UTENSIL: Shallow pan or foil

4 *medium onions*
Sweet butter
Coarse salt
Freshly ground black pepper

1. Wet the onion skins. Cut a cross in the root end to keep insides from popping out. Place the onions in a pan or on a sheet of foil.
2. Bake in a preheated 350° (177° C) oven for 1 hour or until onions are soft when pressed with fingers. Have butter, salt, and pepper available at the table for self-seasoning.

Carol's note: Small onions will bake in 30 minutes.

MACARONI AND CHEESE CUSTARD

6 side servings;
4 main-course servings

PREPARATION TIME: Less than 30 minutes
COOKING TIME: 35 to 40 minutes
BEST UTENSILS: Medium-sized saucepot; small, deep casserole

1½ *cups elbow macaroni*
2 *large eggs*
1 *cup milk*
1 *teaspoon salt*
1 *cup grated or finely cut cheddar cheese*

1. Boil the macaroni in the saucepot in 3 quarts (2.8 liters) water. Add a teaspoon of salt and a few drops of oil to water. Cook macaroni at a rapid boil until it tastes tender but not quite done (about 10 minutes). It will finish cooking in the oven.

2. Whirl the eggs, milk, and salt in the blender, or mix together with a rotary beater.

3. Generously butter the bottom and sides of the casserole to keep the macaroni from sticking. Layer half the macaroni, sprinkle over half the cheese, pour over half the egg-milk mixture, then repeat layers: macaroni, cheese, and the rest of custard.

4. Bake in a preheated 350° (177° C) oven for 35 to 40 minutes, or until custard is set and a knife inserted in the center comes out clean.

TURK'S NOODLES WITH COTTAGE CHEESE

4 side servings;
2 main servings

Plan as a hot companion with roast meats, or enjoy hot or cold as a light, lazy summer dinner, followed by cool fresh fruit.

PREPARATION TIME: Under 10 minutes
COOKING TIME: Under 15 minutes
BEST UTENSIL: Large kettle

1 pound (454 g) broad egg noodles
16 ounces (454 g) California-style cottage cheese
or
½ pint (227 g) sour cream
1 lemon

1. Bring 5 to 6 quarts of water to a boil. Add 2 teaspoons salt and a few drops of oil to the water. Add noodles. Boil vigorously for 7 minutes or until a tasted noodle is tender.

2. Drain the noodles in a colander. Transfer back to the pot and mix in the cottage cheese or sour cream. If needed, reheat on very low heat. Squeeze on lemon juice, the Turkish touch.

PASTA

6 side servings;
3 or 4 main-course servings

Search out and stock up on imported Italian pasta.

PREPARATION TIME: 5 minutes
COOKING TIME: Under 15 minutes
BEST UTENSIL: Large kettle

1 pound (454 g) pasta noodles
2 tablespoons salt
1 tablespoon oil
Sauce of your choice (see next three recipes)

1. Bring 6 quarts (6 liters) of water to a boil. (Cover pot for quick action.) Add the salt and oil.

2. When the water is boiling rapidly, add the noodles. Hold pasta in one hand, then lower into water. As the pasta begins to soften in the water, push the noodles down until they are all submerged.

3. Boil, uncovered, 9 to 12 minutes or until the pasta is tender but still firm. Stir once or twice during cooking time. Pull out a test strand with tongs. Drain pasta in a colander, then return to the pot or a serving bowl and sauce immediately to keep pasta from sticking together.

GARLIC AND OIL SAUCE

enough for 1 pound pasta

PREPARATION TIME: Under 15 minutes
COOKING TIME: Under 10 minutes
BEST UTENSIL: Small skillet or saucepot

¾ cup olive oil
4 large garlic cloves, chopped
Coarse salt to taste

1. Heat the oil and garlic over low heat just until the garlic starts to brown.

2. Pour over hot drained pasta. Salt. Mix well.

Carol's note: For Garlic, Oil, and Anchovy Sauce, add a drained 2-ounce (57-g) tin of flat anchovies, cut into small pieces. Omit salt from ingredients.

EASIEST TOMATO SAUCE

PREPARATION TIME: 5 minutes
COOKING TIME: 45 minutes
BEST UTENSIL: Medium-sized saucepot

3 8-ounce (237 ml) cans tomato sauce
1 6-ounce (177 ml) can tomato paste
1 cup dry red wine
1 large garlic clove, pressed
½ teaspoon oregano
1 tablespoon olive oil

1. Bring the tomato sauce, tomato paste, wine, garlic, oregano, and olive oil to a boiling point over medium heat. Cover the pot, reduce heat to low, and simmer 45 minutes.

Carol's notes: Spoon over hot pasta. Serve with grated Parmesan cheese.

For Mushroom Sauce, add ¼ pound (113 g) fresh sliced mushrooms to pot.

PESTO

enough for 1 pound (454 g) pasta

Pesto is prepared with fresh basil, which may be bought in vegetable markets selling herbs (August is the height of the basil season), grown outdoors from seedlings in a small plot, or in a window box under artificial light. Basil is an herb grown since ancient times; it was cultivated in the gardens of Babylon.

PREPARATION TIME: Under 10 minutes
COOKING TIME: None
BEST UTENSIL: Food processor or blender

2 cups fresh basil leaves, packed down
½ cup olive oil
2 cloves garlic
½ cup pine nuts (pignoli)
⅓ cup grated Parmesan cheese
1 teaspoon salt

1. Wash the basil leaves with cold water. Discard tough stems.

2. Put all the ingredients into a food processor or a blender. (Garlic should be coarsely chopped for blender.) Whirl until well mixed. Pesto should have the consistency of mayonnaise. Add more oil if it is too thick. Stir before using, as it darkens with exposure to the air.

Carol's note: Pesto is wonderful on cold tomatoes or hot potatoes.

The potato was cultivated in South America long before Europe discovered the "New Continent."

Pictorial representations of potatoes appear on pottery from A.D. 2. Methods for dehydrating potatoes have been known since prehistoric times.

The first potatoes were sent from America to Spain by one of Pizarro's officers. Eventually, the potato reached the Pope; he sent the tuber for examination to a botanist, who called it a "little truffle." Even so, throughout Europe *Solanum tuberosum* was used mainly for feeding cattle and prisoners.

It was in a German prison that Antoine Auguste Parmentier, a pharmacist captured from the French Army, first tasted the potato. Liberated and back in Paris, Parmentier tried to popularize the potato but was severely criticized. While he worked as a pharmacist at the Hôtel des Invalides, he was forced to resign when he was accused of feeding the government pensioners potatoes.

Privately, Parmentier was persistent about the potato's value. At a dinner party that included Antoine Lavoisier (he first measured the calorie) and Benjamin Franklin, Parmentier served potatoes prepared twenty different ways.

Finally, in 1786, at the banquet to celebrate the birthday of Louis XVI, the king himself acknowledged Parmentier's dedication by publicly accepting from him a bouquet of tiny purple potato flowers. In an emotional moment, the king gave one flower back to Parmentier, put one on his own lapel, and then pinned a flower on his queen, Marie Antoinette.

BAKED SWEET POTATOES

4 to 6 servings

PREPARATION TIME: 5 minutes
COOKING TIME: 1 hour

4 to 6 medium-sized sweet potatoes
Butter
Coarse salt
Freshly ground black pepper

1. Wash the sweet potatoes well. Rub off brown spots with a vegetable brush. Stab each potato in two places with the tines of a fork.

2. Arrange the potatoes directly on oven rack. Bake in a preheated 350° (177° C) oven for 1 hour or until potatoes are soft to the touch or easily pierced with fork tines.

3. Slit the potatoes, squeeze open, then fluff up inside with fork. Have butter, salt, and pepper available to diners.

SAFFRON POTATOES

4 servings

PREPARATION TIME: 20 minutes
COOKING TIME: 1 hour
BEST UTENSIL: Small casserole with lid

4 large red potatoes, peeled and cubed
(4 or 5 cups: red potatoes are waxy, not mealy, and do not crumble when cooked)
½ teaspoon saffron threads
1¼ cups hot chicken broth
1 large garlic clove, pressed
¼ cup olive oil
½ teaspoon coarse salt, or salt to taste

1. Dissolve the saffron threads in the chicken broth. Add the garlic.

2. Put the potato cubes into the casserole. Pour saffron broth over. Bake, covered, in a preheated 350° (177° C) for 55 minutes. Stir in the olive oil to coat potatoes. Add the salt. Cover and bake 5 more minutes or until the potatoes are completely tender.

Carol's notes: If potatoes are peeled in advance, cover with cold water to retain color.

To double recipe, use a medium-sized casserole.

ESTHER'S SWEET POTATO PIE

6 servings

On more than one Thanksgiving Day morning I have phoned my mother long distance for her recipe. I'm glad it's finally written down.

PREPARATION TIME: 30 minutes
COOKING TIME: 45 minutes' boiling time; 45 minutes' baking time
BEST UTENSILS: Medium-sized saucepan; 9- to 10-inch (23- to 25-cm) pie plate

4 *large sweet potatoes*
1 *8-ounce (227-g) can crushed pineapple, drained*
1 *large egg*
½ *cup orange juice (approximately)*
Marshmallows (about 24)

1. Boil the sweet potatoes in their skins, covered, for about 45 minutes. Cool slightly before handling, then slip skins off. While warm, mash in a large bowl with potato masher.

2. Mix in the crushed pineapple, egg, and enough orange juice to moisten. Spoon into a 9- or 10-inch (23- to 25-cm) pie

plate and bake in a 350° (177° C) oven for 35 minutes or until pie is hot throughout. Cover completely with the marshmallows, return to the oven, and bake until marshmallows have melted into a crust (about 10 minutes).

Carol's note: For show, the potato mixture may be stuffed into scooped-out orange halves and baked in a shallow pan.

BAKED POTATOES

1 to 8 servings

PREPARATION TIME: 5 minutes
COOKING TIME: About 1¼ hours

1 to 8 portion-sized baking potatoes (for timing, choose the same size)

1. Scrub the potatoes with a vegetable brush under cold running water. Stab the potatoes once or twice with fork tines to allow steam to escape.
2. Put the potatoes directly on oven rack. At 350° (177° C), potatoes take approximately 1¼ hours.
3. Slit the potatoes, then squeeze open. Serve with butter or sour cream. I like mine plain, with coarse salt and freshly ground black pepper.

Carol's notes: Baking potato nails are aluminum skewers that conduct heat through the potato and reduce baking time by about 15 minutes.

A radar range will bake a potato impressively in 3 to 4 minutes, but potatoes will not be crisp.

ANN'S POTATOES ANNA

4 servings

PREPARATION TIME: Under 30 minutes
COOKING TIME: 45 minutes
BEST UTENSIL: Glass pie plate (Glass cooks faster than other utensils.)

4 large potatoes, peeled
Coarse salt
Freshly ground black pepper
4 ounces (113 g) butter (1 stick), melted
Sweet Hungarian paprika

1. Slice the potatoes very thin. Butter the sides and bottom of the pie plate.

2. Layer the potatoes in a circle, slightly overlapping each potato disk. Season with salt and pepper. Pour over ⅓ of the melted butter. Repeat layers twice more: potatoes, salt, pepper, and butter. End with a sprinkle of sweet Hungarian paprika.

3. Bake in a 400° (204° C) oven for 45 minutes or until the potatoes are tender, brown, and crisp. If there is too much butter in the dish for potatoes to crisp, spoon it out.

BOILED OR OVEN-BROWNED POTATOES

4 to 6 servings

PREPARATION TIME: Under 15 minutes
COOKING TIME: About 40 minutes
BEST UTENSIL: Large saucepot or top-of-stove casserole

4 to 6 medium-sized potatoes (if large, cut in half)
1 teaspoon salt

1. Scrub the potatoes with a vegetable brush under cold running water. Put into pot and cover with waterAdd the salt.

2. Bring water to a boil over high heat, then reduce heat to medium, cover pot, and gently boil potatoes for about 40 minutes, or until potatoes are tender throughout when carefully tested with fork tines or the blade of a paring knife.

3. Drain the potatoes. Skins will slip off easily. Use a paper napkin to handle hot potatoes. Keep warm over low heat, or on a hot tray.

For Oven-Browned Potatoes:

Boil potatoes 15 to 20 minutes. Peel, then cut into halves or quarters. Add to roasting meat or fowl. Turn several times during cooking to coat with pan fat. At 325° to 350° (163° to 177° C), potatoes take about 1 hour.

Carol's note: Boil small new potatoes in salted water for 20 to 25 minutes. Drain. Roll in butter and freshly snipped dill. According to size, allow 3 or 4 per person.

EASIEST RICE

4 servings

Rice steamed in the oven emerges fluffy and dry, with each grain perfectly separated.

PREPARATION TIME: 5 minutes
COOKING TIME: 30 minutes
BEST UTENSIL: Small deep casserole with lid

1 cup (227 g) raw rice
1 teaspoon salt
2 cups water

1. Put the rice, salt, and water in the casserole. Cover and bake in a 350° (177° C) oven for 30 minutes. Stir, re-cover, and cook 5 more minutes or until all liquid is absorbed.

Carol's notes: Use 2 cups of beef or chicken broth in place of water. Omit salt.

Allow 45 minutes if oven temperature is set at 325° (163° C).

SAFFRON RICE WITH RAISINS AND ALMONDS

4 servings

PREPARATION TIME: Under 15 minutes
COOKING TIME: 30 to 45 minutes
BEST UTENSIL: Small deep casserole

2½ cups mild chicken broth
½ teaspoon saffron threads
⅓ cup golden raisins
½ teaspoon coarse salt
1 cup (227 g) raw rice
½ cup slivered almonds

1. Make chicken broth with 2 teaspoons powdered chicken base mixed with 2½ cups boiling water. Add the saffron, raisins (to plump), and salt. Let stand 10 to 15 minutes.

2. Put the rice and the almonds into casserole. Pour saffron broth over rice. Cover casserole and steam in a 350° (177° C) oven for 30 minutes. Fluff rice, re-cover, and steam 5 more minutes or until rice is tender.

Carol's note: Allow 45 minutes in a 325° (163° C) oven.

SAUTÉED FRESH SPINACH

4 servings

PREPARATION TIME: 15 to 20 minutes
COOKING TIME: Under 10 minutes
BEST UTENSIL: Large skillet

2 pounds (.9 kg) loose spinach (look for crisp, dark green, unyellowed leaves)
3 tablespoons peanut oil
2 teaspoons Japanese soy sauce
½ teaspoon red wine vinegar

1. Soak the spinach in a bowl of lukewarm water. Drain, then rinse under cold running water. Slice off thick, tough stems. Discard bruised or brown leaves. Pat dry with paper towels or dry in a salad spinner.

2. Heat the oil over medium high heat. When a drop of water spatters in the pan, add all the spinach to the skillet.

3. Fry, stirring constantly until the spinach leaves are wilted and coated with oil. Turn down heat to low and cook for 2 more minutes. Add the soy sauce and vinegar. Stir and serve.

ACORN SQUASH

4 servings

Sweet-meated, filling, warming winter squash baked in its edible skin.

PREPARATION TIME: 10 minutes
COOKING TIME: 45 minutes
BEST UTENSIL: Shallow baking pan

1 medium-sized acorn squash
2 ounces (57 g) butter (½ stick)
Sugar
Coarse salt
Freshly ground black pepper

1. With a sturdy knife, cut the squash in half across the fat middle. Scoop out seeds.

2. Fill center hollows with the butter. Season with sugar, salt, and pepper. Put into baking dish, hollow side up. Pour 1 inch (2.5 cm) water into the bottom of the pan.

3. Bake in a preheated 350° (177° C) oven for 45 minutes or until squash meat is soft throughout when pierced with fork tines. During cooking time, baste rims of squash twice with butter–sugar mixture from hollows. Add water to pan if it evaporates.

BUTTER-BAKED ZUCCHINI IN FOIL

4 servings

Every diner gets an individual squash package.

PREPARATION TIME: 10 minutes
COOKING TIME: 20 minutes
BEST UTENSIL: Aluminum foil

4 small zucchini (about 1 pound, or 454 g)
(look for unspotted, shiny-skinned ones)
Butter
Coarse salt
Freshly ground black pepper

1. Wash the zucchini, pat dry, then slice into ½-inch (1.3-cm) pieces.

2. Arrange each sliced squash on an ample square of foil. Dot with butter. Season with salt and pepper. Wrap securely.

3. Bake directly on oven rack or in a shallow pan in a preheated 350° (177° C) oven for 20 minutes.

SAUERKRAUT IN BEER

4 servings

PREPARATION TIME: 10 minutes
COOKING TIME: 1 hour
BEST UTENSIL: Small top-of-stove casserole

- 2 *pounds (908 g) fresh sauerkraut*
- 1 *12-ounce (355-ml) bottle of beer*
- 6 *juniper berries*
- 2 *teaspoons coarse salt*
- ¼ *teaspoon onion powder*

1. Rinse the sauerkraut in a colander under cold running water. Separate strands.

2. Put the sauerkraut, beer, juniper berries, salt, and onion powder into the casserole. Mix well.

3. Cover and simmer over low heat for 1 hour. Stir occasionally (about every 15 minutes).

Carol's note: Convert to a main dish by adding 4 large knackwurst or 8 hot dogs to the pot. Steam sausages for 30 minutes or until they are hot throughout.

WATERCRESS AND SCALLION SALAD

4 to 6 servings

This herb of the mustard family gets its name because it grows in and around water.

PREPARATION TIME: 15 minutes
COOKING TIME: None

2 *bunches watercress*
(slice the tough stem ends from the cress while it is still bunched)
¼ *cup wine vinegar or lemon juice*
¼ *cup olive oil*
½ *teaspoon coarse salt*
⅛ *teaspoon freshly ground black pepper*
1 *small clove garlic, pressed*
6 *scallions, dewhiskered, peeled, and sliced thin*

1. Perk up the watercress by soaking in ice water (water and ice cubes in a bowl) for 15 minutes. Change the water if cress is very dirty. Drain and dry in a salad spinner or roll loosely in paper towels. Refrigerate cress until tossing time.

2. Mix together the vinegar or lemon juice, olive oil, salt, pepper, and pressed garlic. Dressing should barely coat greens.

3. Put cress in salad bowl. Sprinkle scallions over. Toss with dressing just before serving, as watercress is delicate and wilts quickly.

VIII. Desserts

EASIEST CHEESECAKE
PECAN CRACKER PIE
LEMON SOUFFLÉ
GRACE'S CHOCOLATE MOUSSE
ICED CREAM
BRANDIED BANANAS
AUNT HELEN'S CHINESE NOODLE COOKIES
VANILLA ICE CREAM WITH GREEN CHARTREUSE
FRIEDA'S HEAVENLY HASH CAKE
ROSE'S LACE COOKIES
STRAWBERRIES IN KIRSCH
GREEN GRAPES IN SOUR CREAM
TORREJA
SUSAN'S LEMON POUND CAKE
ZABAGLIONE
LARRY'S TOLL HOUSE PIE

At a friend's party, a woman boasted to me that during her trip to Vienna, a city known for pastry without parallel, she had been faithful to her latest reducing diet, restraining herself from sampling any Viennese sweets. Her triumph was the resistance of Sachertorte while dining at the restaurant which bears the name Sacher.

"I suppose it was foolish," she confided. "I gained back the weight anyway."

Sweets are not my passion. My opinions on the dangers of excessive sugar in the diet are expressed in *The Diet Book,* but to dine at Sacher and shun their celebrated torte is foolish.

Someday when I travel to Vienna, I imagine an evening of joyful waltzes, after which I shall go to the Sacher Hotel and order two Sachertortes, one for me and one for the woman who missed the experience.

EASIEST CHEESECAKE

8 generous servings

I gave this recipe to my friend, screenwriter Carl Gottlieb, who spent a glorious week away from his desk, preparing meals for a dozen people on a yacht race from Los Angeles to Mazatlán, Mexico.

Carl logged the Cheesecake triumphant, baked and eaten in the middle of tossing, turbulent waters.

PREPARATION TIME: Under 30 minutes
COOKING TIME: 1 hour
BEST UTENSIL: Approximately 8×10×3-inch (20×25×8-cm) baking pan

4 8-ounce (227-g) packages cream cheese, softened
1 pint (454 g) sour cream
4 large eggs
1½ cups sugar
¾ milk
4 teaspoons unsifted flour
2 teaspoons pure orange extract

1. Blend the softened cream cheese with the sour cream, eggs, sugar, milk, flour, and orange extract. Mix together with a food processor, a masher, or a large fork. The mixture should be smooth and light. Pour into baking pan.

2. Bake in a preheated 350° (177° C) oven for 1 hour. Cool first for 2 or 3 hours, then chill in refrigerator.

Carol's notes: The recipe may be halved.

Cake rises during cooking, then flattens down as it cools.

PECAN CRACKER PIE

PREPARATION TIME: Under 45 minutes
COOKING TIME: 45 minutes
BEST UTENSILS: Electric rotary beater, 9- or 10-inch (23- to 25-cm) pie plate

3 egg whites, at room temperature
½ teaspoon cream of tartar
1 cup sugar
1 teaspoon vanilla
¾ cup chopped pecans
10 squares salted soda crackers, crushed (food processor excels at this, or whirl in a blender; Great Grandma did it with a rolling pin)
Whipped cream

Have all ingredients at arm's length before beginning.

1. Beat the egg whites stiff with a rotary beater. It takes about 10 minutes for whites to stand in peaks.

2. Add the sugar and the cream of tartar. Beat in. Add the vanilla and the nuts. Beat in. Remove the beaters and fold the cracker crumbs in by hand, using a wooden spoon.

3. Press mixture into a well-buttered pie plate. Bake in a

preheated 300° (149° C) oven for 45 minutes. The pie doesn't rise. Cool at room temperature for at least an hour. Top with whipped cream.

Whipped Cream

PREPARATION TIME: Under 15 minutes
COOKING TIME: None
BEST UTENSIL: Electric rotary beater

½ *pint (237 ml) heavy sweet cream, chilled*
2 *tablespoons sugar*
¼ *teaspoon vanilla*

Put the cream into a deep bowl, turn on beaters, and whip. When mixture begins to thicken, add the sugar and vanilla. Turn beaters down to low and continue whipping until cream is the right consistency.

Carol's note: A hand rotary beater whips well, but it certainly isn't "easiest." A blender will whip cream, but the volume of whipped cream is considerably diminished.

LEMON SOUFFLÉ

4 servings

Easy to swallow. One portion has 107 calories, and 8 grams of carbohydrate.

PREPARATION TIME: 20 minutes
COOKING TIME: Under 15 minutes
BEST UTENSILS: Small soufflé dish or casserole; electric rotary beater

4 *large eggs, separated*
2 *tablespoons sugar*
Juice and grated rind of 1 medium-sized lemon

1. Beat the egg yolks well with the sugar, lemon juice, and grated lemon rind.

2. Ten minutes before the soufflé is baked; whip the egg whites until stiff enough to stand in peaks. Fold the egg whites into the lemon and egg mixture.

3. Pour into a buttered baking dish and bake in a preheated 350° (177° C) oven. Let rise for 10 to 12 minutes, or until a knife inserted through the center comes out clean. Serve right away before soufflé cools and collapses.

GRACE'S CHOCOLATE MOUSSE

6 servings

The mousse of Ms. Elmaleh is cleverly concocted, resulting in a hedonistic chocolate froth.

PREPARATION TIME: 30 minutes
COOKING TIME: About 10 minutes to melt chocolate
BEST UTENSILS: Double boiler; electric rotary beater

12 *ounces (340 g) sweet chocolate (of good quality; Baker's German Sweet is one choice)*
8 *large eggs*
2 *tablespoons Grand Marnier*

For the Topping

1 *pint (474 ml) heavy cream*
1 *tablespoon sugar*

1. Break the chocolate into natural divisions. Melt over low heat in the double boiler, stirring occasionally with a wooden spoon.

2. While chocolate is melting, separate the eggs into two large bowls.

3. Beat the egg whites with an electric rotary beater until they are stiff enough to stand in peaks. (Turn off motor to

test.) Set aside for a moment. (Beating egg whites before yolks saves washing the beaters.)

4. Work quickly now. Beat the egg yolks with the Grand Marnier. Add the completely melted chocolate and beat until mixture is smooth.

5. Fold in the egg whites. Mixture will be loose. Refrigerate 2 hours. Before serving, top with the heavy cream whipped and whirled with the sugar in the blender or stiffened by electric rotary beater for more volume.

Carol's note: Must be eaten the day it is made.

ICED CREAM

4 or 5 servings

PREPARATION TIME: 15 minutes
COOKING TIME: None
BEST UTENSIL: Electric rotary beater

½ *pint (237 ml) heavy cream, chilled*
2 *tablespoons sugar*
1 *teaspoon vanilla extract*
½ *cup pecans (about 2½ ounces), ground (grind in food processor or blender)*

1. Whip the cream with an electric rotary beater in a deep bowl. When the cream starts to thicken, add the sugar and vanilla. Whip until the cream stands in stiff peaks when beater is raised from bowl. (Turn off motor first.)

2. Fold in the ground nuts. Spoon into an ice cube tray. Freeze. Defrost 10 to 15 minutes before eating.

Carol's note: Recipe may be doubled and spooned into an 8×8×2-inch (20×20×5-cm) cake pan. The cream may be whipped with a manual rotary beater. Add 10 minutes to the preparation time.

BRANDIED BANANAS

1 to 6 servings

PREPARATION TIME: 10 minutes
COOKING TIME: 20 minutes
BEST UTENSIL: Shallow baking dish

1 to 6 bananas
Sugar
Butter
Brandy (about 1 tablespoon per banana)
Chopped walnuts or pecans

1. Cut peeled banana or bananas in half, then slice lengthwise to yield 4 pieces per banana.
2. Arrange the banana slices in baking dish in one layer. Lightly sprinkle with sugar, dot with butter, douse with brandy, and scatter nuts over all.
3. Bake in a preheated 250° (121° C) oven for 20 minutes.

Carol's note: Easiest to prepare in advance, then slip into the oven toward the finish of the main course.

AUNT HELEN'S CHINESE NOODLE COOKIES

About 25 cookies

Helen Gelfand is a spirited hostess who enjoys asking guests if they know what ingredient makes this cookie's crunch.

PREPARATION TIME: About 30 minutes
COOKING TIME: None
BEST UTENSILS: Saucepot or double boiler; cookie sheet

1 12-ounce (340-g) package semi-sweet chocolate chips
1 6-ounce (170-g) package semi-sweet chocolate chips
2 3-ounce (85-g) cans Chinese noodles
½ cup chopped pecans (about 2 ounces)
½ teaspoon vanilla extract

1. Melt the chips in a pot over very low heat or in the top of a double boiler.

2. Stir together the melted chocolate and noodles until they are well mixed. Stir in the nuts and vanilla.

3. Drop heaping teaspoons of cookie mixture onto a buttered cookie sheet. Cool. When completely cool, refrigerate for 15 minutes only to firm the chocolate. Remove and store in plastic bag.

Carol's note: The cookies may be made with butterscotch-flavored chips.

VANILLA ICE CREAM WITH GREEN CHARTREUSE

4 servings

Green chartreuse is a potent liqueur, made exclusively by French Carthusian monks.

PREPARATION TIME: 5 minutes

1 pint vanilla ice cream
Green chartreuse

Top individual scoops or slices of vanilla ice cream with 2 or 3 tablespoons green chartreuse.

FRIEDA'S HEAVENLY HASH CAKE

10 to 12 servings

Frieda's formidable dessert loosens all belts at least one notch.

PREPARATION TIME: 30 minutes
COOKING TIME: None
BEST UTENSILS: Saucepot or double boiler; approximately 9 × 12-inch (23 × 30-cm) baking dish; electric rotary beater

1 *large (10-inch, or 25-cm) angel food cake*
16 *ounces (454 g) semi-sweet chocolate chips*
½ *envelope unflavored Knox gelatin dissolved in 2 tablespoons water*
4 *large eggs*
1 *pint (474 ml) heavy cream*
1 *tablespoon sugar*
1 *cup chopped pecans*

1. Break angel food cake into pieces the size of walnuts.

2. Melt the chocolate chips in a double boiler or a saucepot set over low heat. Cool slightly. Mix the dissolved gelatin with the melted chips. An electric rotary beater is helpful in this and the following operation.

3. In a separate bowl, beat the eggs until foamy, then mix the egg and melted chocolate together thoroughly.

4. Whirl ½ pint heavy cream in a blender until it is thickened. Fold into chocolate mixture.

5. For the topping, whirl remaining ½ pint cream and the sugar in the blender until it is thick, or beat until thick with an electric rotary beater for more volume.

6. Butter the bottom of the baking dish, then add a layer of angel food cake pieces. Pour half the chocolate mixture over cake, then add another layer of cake and the rest of the

chocolate mixture. Spread the cake with the pint of whipped cream topping and sprinkle with the nuts. Cover with foil and chill thoroughly.

Carol's notes: Best made the day before, allowing time for cake to saturate chocolate and whipped cream.

Remove from refrigerator ½ hour before serving.

ROSE'S LACE COOKIES

Courtesy of my mother-in-law.

PREPARATION TIME: 15 minutes
COOKING TIME: Under 15 minutes per batch
BEST UTENSILS: Cookie sheet; aluminum foil

1 *cup quick-cooking oats*
¾ *cup sugar*
3 *tablespoons unsifted flour*
1 *teaspoon salt*
4 *ounces (113 g) butter (1 stick), melted*
1 *large egg, beaten*
2 *teaspoons vanilla*

1. In a large bowl, combine the oats, sugar, flour, and salt.

2. Mix in the melted butter, beaten egg, and vanilla.

3. Place foil on cookie sheet. Drop on very small amounts (about ¼ teaspoon). Arrange cookies about 2½ inches apart.

4. Bake in a preheated 350° (177° C) oven for 10 to 12 minutes or until cookies have spread and are lightly browned. Let cool for several minutes, then lift cookies off foil. Same sheet of foil may be used for several batches.

STRAWBERRIES IN KIRSCH

6 servings

Kirschwasser is cherry brandy.

PREPARATION TIME: 15 minutes
COOKING TIME: None

2 *pint baskets of fresh strawberries*
2 *tablespoons sugar*
6 *tablespoons kirsch*

1. Wash the berries in a colander, then hull (remove the stem) with a strawberry huller, or the tip of a sharp parig knife.

2. Slice the strawberries into a large bowl. Gently stir in the sugar and kirsch. Refrigerate for 2 hours. Spoon into individual bowls and serve.

GREEN GRAPES IN SOUR CREAM

Serves 6

Old faithful.

PREPARATION TIME: 10 minutes
COOKING TIME: None

1 *pound (454 g) fresh seedless green grapes (about 2 cups: look for pale, unbruised little fingernail-sized grapes)*
¼ *cup dark brown sugar*
½ *pint (227 g) commercial sour cream*

1. Wash the grapes well, then pluck them from their stems.

2. In a large bowl, mix and coat the grapes with the brown sugar and sour cream. Chill well before serving.

TORREJA

4 servings

Cuban in origin. Triples as breakfast or late-night snack.

PREPARATION TIME: 15 minutes
COOKING TIME: Under 15 minutes
BEST UTENSIL: 12-inch (30-cm) skillet

8 to 10 slices Italian or French bread, hardened
Milk or wine
2 large eggs
2 ounces (57 g) butter (½ stick)
1 tablespoon peanut oil
Maple syrup, or your favorite fruit preserves

1. Moisten the bread by dipping it into milk or wine. Dip both sides of each slice in the beaten eggs.

2. Heat the butter and oil over medium heat until a drop of water splatters in the pan. Fry the bread slices for 4 or 5 minutes on each side, turning with a spatula. Add more butter if necessary. Serve with maple syrup or preserves.

SUSAN'S LEMON POUND CAKE

Susan Gurney teaches home economics and should grade herself A+ for this creation.

PREPARATION TIME: 15 to 30 minutes
COOKING TIME: 1½ hours
BEST UTENSILS: Food processor or portable electric mixer; 10-inch (25-cm) tube pan

All ingredients should be at room temperature.

8 *ounces (227 g) sweet butter (2 sticks)*
½ *cup peanut oil*
3 *cups sugar*
5 *eggs*
1 *cup milk*
3 *cups flour, unsifted*
1 *teaspoon baking powder*
½ *teaspoon salt*
2 *tablespoons pure lemon extract*

1. Blend the butter and oil in a food processor, or in a large bowl with a portable electric mixer.

2. Add the sugar and blend.

3. Add the eggs one at a time. Then add the milk.

4. Add the flour, baking powder, salt, and lemon extract. Blend in.

5. Pour into a tube baking pan that has been buttered and sprinkled with flour. Bake in a cold (not preheated) oven at 325° (163° C) for 1½ hours. Let cool, then remove cake from pan and refrigerate, where it will keep for a week.

Carol's notes: If using a food processor, the container will be full.

If using an electric rotary beater, the entire cake may be made in one bowl, adding ingredients and blending them without removing beaters.

For lemon-strawberry pound cake, spoon sliced, sugared, chilled fresh strawberries over cake. Top with freshly whipped cream.

ZABAGLIONE

4 servings

The classic Italian pudding sweetened with Marsala wine. Ambrosial warm; OK cold.

PREPARATION TIME: Under 15 minutes
COOKING TIME: Under 10 minutes
BEST UTENSILS: Double boiler; electric rotary beater

6 *egg yolks*
3 *tablespoons sugar*
½ *cup dry Marsala wine*

1. Pour water into bottom of double boiler, making sure it does not touch bottom of top pot. Place pan over medium-low heat. Water should not boil.

2. Combine the egg yolks, sugar, and Marsala in top of double boiler. Beat with electric mixer at low speed until pudding is fluffy and has thickened enough to stand in soft peaks. (Turn off the motor to test.) This takes at least 5 minutes, so be patient.

Carol's note: Very pretty served in champagne glasses.

LARRY'S TOLL HOUSE PIE

6 servings

Larry Weiss mixes up this incredibly rich chocolate-nut batter by hand, but it's easiest to plug in a portable electric beater.

PREPARATION TIME: 20 minutes
COOKING TIME: 1 hour
BEST UTENSIL: 9-inch (23-cm) pie plate

- 2 *large eggs*
- ½ *cup unsifted flour*
- 1 *cup sugar*
- 1 *teaspoon vanilla*
- 4 *ounces (113 g) sweet butter (1 stick), melted*
- 1¼ *cups chopped walnuts*
- 1¼ *cups semi-sweet chocolate chips*
- 9- *inch (23-cm) pie shell*
  (I found several brands of frozen pie shells made with unbleached flour and honey—bravo!)
  Whipped cream

1. Beat the eggs well in a large, deep bowl. Add the flour and sugar and beat until well blended. Add the vanilla and melted butter. Beat until all ingredients are mixed thoroughly.

2. Mix in the nuts and chocolate chips by hand, with a wooden spoon. Spread the batter in the pie plate.

3. Bake in a preheated 350° (177° C) oven for 1 hour. A crust will form on top. Cool. Top with freshly whipped cream before serving.

Index